Nimue

Crochet Blanket
by Shelley Husband

*A crochet quest
of epic proportions*

Copyright © 2022 by Shelley Husband

All rights reserved. No part of this publication may be reproduced or transmitted by any means, electronic, photocopying or otherwise without prior written permission of the author.

ISBN-13: 978-0-6451573-6-9

Charts by Amy Gunderson

Email: kinglouiespizza@gmail.com
Ravelry ID: AmyGunderson

Graphic Design by Michelle Lorimer

Email: hello@michellelorimer.com

Blanket Photography by Jo O'Keefe

Email: jookeefe@hotmail.com
Instagram: missfarmerjojo

Other Photography by Shelley Husband

Technical Editing by SiewBee Pond

Email: essbee1995@yahoo.com

First edition 2022

Published by Shelley Husband
PO Box 11
Narrawong VIC 3285
Australia

shelleyhusbandcrochet.com

0824

CONTENTS

Provisions for Your Adventure
6

Navigating Nimue
13

Avalon Pattern	*Caltha Pattern*	*Nimue Pattern*
14	**26**	**28**

Avalon Charts	*Caltha Charts*	*Nimue Charts*
36	**39**	**40**

Nimue's Counsel
43

Avalon	*Caltha*	*Nimue*
44	**89**	**94**

Nimue's Tidings
117

Glossary	*Left-handed Charts*	*Helpful Links*
118	**120**	**127**

Thank You
128

About the Author &
Other Books by Shelley Husband
129

WELCOME TO THE
QUEST FOR NIMUE

Dive into the waters of the Lady of the Lake, sometimes known as Nimue, a character of the Arthurian legends.

She has been known by many names and played varied roles in the multitude of tales of King Arthur. Most commonly, she is the Lady of the Lake - custodian of Excalibur. She is a seer, a guardian - mysterious and powerful. Guiding or thwarting the more well-known characters in their quests.

And so, Nimue will use her powers of prescience to guide you on your quest. She has scried the future and knows the times you will face hardships and has wise counsel ready to guide you. While you will encounter challenges as you progress, there are many tranquil sections to rest between adventures. Nimue will ensure you survive the adventure with quietude. She has foreseen the future and can sense the wonder you will create.

You will begin your crusade with mystical Avalon before traversing the misty boundaries of the isle with Caltha and concluding with Nimue herself in all her glory.

Ready your steed and provisions, for 'tis time to begin your quest. May the road ahead be smooth.

Provisions
for your quest

The information provided here will give you all you need to know to source your yarn. You can use any yarn. To successfully use a yarn other than what I have used, compare the metres per gram ratio. If your yarn has more meters per gram, you will have ample. If it has less, you will need more yarn that what is stated here.

Your crochet style and hook size will also impact the amount of yarn you use. If you want more drape and use a larger hook, you will need more yarn. If you want a tighter fabric and use a smaller hook, you will need less.

One colour Nimue

Bendigo Woollen Mills Cotton
4 ply/sock/fingering

Metres/yards per gram: 3.35/3.66
Hook: 3.5 mm
Blanket size: 130 cm/51 in
Total amount needed: 3,803 metres/4,159 yards/6 balls

Bendigo Woollen Mills Cotton
8 ply/DK/light worsted

Metres/yards per gram: 2.43/2.66
Hook: 4.5 mm
Blanket size: 158 cm/62 in
Total amount needed: 4,183 metres/4,575 yards/9 balls

Bendigo Woollen Mills Cotton
10 ply/aran/worsted

Metres/yards per gram: 1.80/1.97
Hook: 5.5 mm
Estimated Blanket size: 185 cm/73 in
Total amount needed: 5,020 metres/5,490 yards/14 balls

Blues Nimue

Made while taking the Help photos and videos included, this version changes colour every round.

Avalon

Use Parchment for odd numbered rounds. Alternate between French Navy and Blue Ice for the even numbered rounds.

Caltha

Use Parchment for even numbered rounds. Begin with French Navy and alternate with Blue Ice for odd numbered rounds.

Nimue

Use Parchment for even numbered rounds. Alternate between French Navy and Blue Ice for odd numbered rounds.

Bendigo Woollen Mills Cotton 4 ply/sock/fingering

Metres/yards per gram: 3.35/3.66
Hook: 3.5 mm
Blanket size: 130 cm/51 in

Amounts and Colours used

Blue Ice: 1,037 metres/1,134 yards/2 balls
French Navy: 954 metres/1,044 yards/2 balls
Parchment: 1,659 metres/1,815 yards/3 balls

Kim's Nimue

Made for me by Kim Siebenhausen, this colourful Nimue shows off pinks and yellow along with my favourite, Parchment. Kim used a smaller hook than I would with the yarn, so her blanket is smaller.

Bendigo Woollen Mills Cotton
10 ply/aran/worsted

Metres/yards per gram: 1.80/1.97
Hook: 4.5 mm
Blanket size: 148 cm/58 in

Amounts and Colours used

Parchment: 2,095 metres/2,291 yards/6 balls
Pink Rose: 863 metres/944 yards/3 balls
Daffodil: 451 metres/493 yards/2 balls
Peach: 410 metres/448 yards/2 balls
Hot Pink: 439 metres/480 yards/2 balls

See page 126 for a table of the colour used for each round.

Luxury Nimue

Made for me by Samantha Taylor, this deliciously lush version of Nimue uses a yarn made with "barber-pole" construction, combining merino wool and Suri alpaca yarns.

Great Ocean Road Woollen Mills Antares merino and Suri alpaca yarn

Metres/yards per gram: 2.00/2.19
Hook: 5 mm
Blanket Size: 168 cm/66 in
Total amount needed: 5,000 metres/5,468 yards/25 skeins

Gauge

Gauge is not really important to match, but if you want to make sure you have enough yarn, here is the size of the Caltha square in each yarn used. If yours matches or is slightly smaller, you will be fine. While I have overestimated the yarn requirements a little, if your Caltha square is larger, you may need more yarn to complete the entire blanket.

>> 4 ply/sock/fingering, 3.5 mm hook:
   11.5 cm/4.5 in

>> 10 ply/aran/worsted, 4.5 mm hook:
   12 cm/4.75 in
   (not pictured)

>> 8 ply/DK/light worsted, 4.5 mm hook:
   13 cm/5 in

>> Great Ocean Road Woollen Mills Antares, 5 mm hook:
   15 cm/6 in

>> 10 ply/aran/worsted, 5.5 mm hook:
   16.5 cm/6.5 in

Nimue's Counsel

Before you begin your adventure, Nimue has some advice for you.

To make your crochet look seamless, work a false stitch instead of a starting chain. While I state the standard starting chain at the beginning of rounds, (e.g. ch3 to take the place of a treble crochet UK terms/double crochet US terms), I rarely use starting chains when crocheting. Instead, I use a false stitch. You can find a video of it on my YouTube Channel linked to on the Helpful Links page.

Tedious as it is, checking your stitch counts match the numbers stated in the pattern will help you avoid traps and pitfalls as you progress.

If you are unsure at any time, refer to the Help pages or the videos. If that fails, please check the Helpful links page to access further help.

Now let's begin our adventure.

NAVIGATING NIMUE

Here you will find the path to follow to complete your quest for Nimue in both written directions and charted maps.

No matter the language you speak, Nimue can communicate the way to you. The UK terminology directions are followed by the US terminology patterns, and then the right-handed charts. Left-handers, you will find the left-hand versions of the charts in Nimue's Tidings towards the end of the book.

Avalon
Granny Square Pattern

UK TERMS

Begin with mc.

R1: ch1, *dc, 5tr*, rep from * to * 3x, join with ss to first st. {24 sts}

R2: ch3 (stch), *ch2, skip 2 sts, dc in next st, ch2, skip 2 sts**, tr in next st*, rep from * to * 2x and * to ** 1x, join with ss to 3rd ch of stch. {8 sts, 8 2-ch sps}

R3: dc in same st as ss, *3dc in 2-ch sp**, dc in next st*, rep from * to * 6x and * to ** 1x, join with ss to first st. {32 sts}

R4: ch3 (stch), tr in same st as ss, *tr in next 3 sts**, 2tr in next st*, rep from * to * 6x and * to ** 1x, join with ss to 3rd ch of stch. {40 sts}

R5: dc in same st as ss, dc in next 39 sts, join with ss to first st. {40 sts}

R6: dc in same st as ss, *ch1, fphdtr around R4 st below next st, ch1, skip 1 st**, dc in next st*, rep from * to * 18x and * to ** 1x, join with ss to first st. {40 sts, 40 1-ch sps}

R7: ch3 (stch), *tr in 1-ch sp, fphdtr around next st, tr in 1-ch sp**, tr in next st*, rep from * to * 18x and * to ** 1x, join with ss to 3rd ch of stch. {80 sts}

R8: dc in same st as ss, *skip 1 st, (fphdtr around, tr in, fphdtr around) next st, skip 1 st**, dc in next st*, rep from * to * 18x and * to ** 1x, join with ss to first st. {80 sts}

R9: **This round will be very ruffled.** ch3 (stch), *(fptr around, tr in) next st, ch1, 5tr in next st, ch1, (tr in, fptr around) next st**, tr in next st*, rep from * to * 18x and * to ** 1x, join with ss to 3rd ch of stch. {200 sts, 40 1-ch sps}

R10: ch1, fpdc around 2 fp sts at the same time skipping st ss'd into, *dc in next st, dc in both 1-ch sps either side of next 5 sts at the same time, dc in next st**, fpdc around next 2 fp sts at the same time skipping st between*, rep from * to * 18x and * to ** 1x, join with ss to first st. {80 sts}

R11: dc in same st as ss, dc in next 79 sts, join with ss to first st. {80 sts}

R12: dc in same st as ss, *ch2, skip 1 st**, dc in next st*, rep from * to * 38x and * to ** 1x, join with ss to first st. {40 sts, 40 2-ch sps}

R13: fpss around st ss'd into, ch3 (stch), ch2, fphdtr around same st as ss, *2tr in 2-ch sp**, (fphdtr around, ch2, fphdtr around) next st*, rep from * to * 38x and * to ** 1x, join with ss to 3rd ch of stch. {160 sts, 40 2-ch sps}

R14: ch3 (stch), *5tr in 2-ch sp, (tr in, fptr around) next st, skip 3 sts, dc in 2-ch sp, skip 3 sts**, (fptr around, tr in) next st*, rep from * to * 18x and * to ** 1x, fptr around next st, join with ss to 3rd ch of stch. {200 sts}

R15: *dc in next 2 sts, 3tr in next st, dc in next 2 sts, skip 1 st, fpdc around next 2 fp sts at the same time skipping st between**, skip 1 st*, rep from * to * 18x and * to ** 1x, do not join. {160 sts}

R16: dc in last st of R15, *ch5, skip 7 sts**, dc in next st*, rep from * to * 18x and * to ** 1x, join with ss to first st. {20 sts, 20 5-ch sps}

R17: ch3 (stch), 3tr in same st as ss, *dc in 5-ch sp**, 7tr in next st*, rep from * to * 18x and * to ** 1x, 3tr in same st as first sts, join with ss to 3rd ch of stch. {160 sts}

R18: ch3 (stch), tr in same st as ss, *2tr in next 3 sts, skip 4 sts, dc in next st, skip 4 sts, 2tr in next 3 sts**, (2tr, ch2, 2tr) in next st*, rep from * to * 8x and * to ** 1x, 2tr in same st as first sts, ch1, join with dc to 3rd ch of stch. {170 sts, 10 2-ch sps}

R19: ch2 (stch), *htr in next 8 sts, ss in next st, htr in next 8 sts**, htr in 2-ch sp*, rep from * to * 8x and * to ** 1x, join with inv join to first true st. {180 sts}

R20: Attach with stdg tr2tog in lbv of the sts either side of any ss, *htr in lbv of next 4 sts, dc in lbv of next 7 sts, htr in lbv of next 4 sts**, tr2tog in lbv of next 3 sts skipping the middle st*, rep from * to * 8x and * to ** 1x, join with ss to first st. {160 sts}

R21: ch3 (stch), *tr in next 2 sts, htr in next 3 sts, dc in next 5 sts, htr in next 3 sts, tr in next 2 sts**, 2tr in next st*, rep from * to * 8x and * to ** 1x, tr in same st as first st, join with ss to 3rd ch of stch. {170 sts}

R22: dc in same st as ss, dc in next 7 sts, *2dc in next st**, dc in next 16 sts*, rep from * to * 8x and * to ** 1x, dc in next 8 sts, join with ss to first st. {180 sts}

R23: ch4, (2dtrcl, ch2, 3dtrcl) in same st as ss, *ch2, skip 1 st, 3dtrcl in next st, skip 3 sts, dc in next 34 sts, skip 3 sts, 3dtrcl in next st, ch2, skip 1 st**, (2x [3dtrcl, ch2], 3dtrcl) in next st*, rep from * to * 2x and * to ** 1x, 3dtrcl in same st as first sts, ch2, join with ss to top of 2dtrcl. {34 sts on each side; 4 (5-st & 4 2-ch sp) cnrs}

R24: ss to 2-ch sp, ch4 (stch), (2dtrcl, ch2, 3dtrcl) in same sp, skip 1 st, 2x [ch2, 3dtrcl] in 2-ch sp, *skip 4 sts, dc in next 28 sts, skip 4 sts**, 3x [(3dtrcl, ch2, 3dtrcl, ch2) in 2-ch sp, skip 1 st], (3dtrcl, ch2, 3dtrcl) in 2-ch sp*, rep from * to * 2x and * to ** 1x, 2x [(3dtrcl, ch2) in 2-ch sp], skip 1 st, (3dtrcl, ch2, 3dtrcl) in 2-ch sp, skip 1 st, ch1, join with dc to top of 2dtrcl. {28 sts on each side; 4 (8-st & 7 2-ch sp) cnrs}

R25: ch4 (stch), (2dtrcl, ch2, 3dtrcl) over joining dc, *3x [ch2, skip 1 st, 3dtrcl] in 2-ch sp, skip 3 sts, dc in next 24 sts, skip 3 sts, 3x [3dtrcl in 2-ch sp, ch2, skip 1 st]**, (2x [3dtrcl, ch2], 3dtrcl) in 2-ch cnr sp*, rep from * to * 2x and * to ** 1x, 3dtrcl in same sp as first sts, ch2, join with ss to top of 2dtrcl. {24 sts on each side; 4 (9-st & 8 2-ch sp) cnrs}

R26: dc in same st as ss, *4x [3dc in 2-ch sp, fpdc around next st], dc between last and next sts, dc in next 24 sts, dc between last and next sts, 4x [fpdc around next st, 3dc in 2-ch sp]**, (dc, ch2, dc) in next st*, rep from * to * 2x and * to ** 1x, dc in same st as first st, ch1, join with dc to first st. {60 sts on each side; 4 2-ch cnr sps}

R27: ch3 (stch), tr over joining dc, *tr in next 60 sts**, 3tr in 2-ch cnr sp*, rep from * to * 2x and * to ** 1x, tr in same sp as first sts, join with ss to 3rd ch of stch. {60 sts on each side; 4 3-st cnrs}

R28: dc in same st as ss, *dc in next 62 sts**, (dc, ch2, dc) in next st*, rep from * to * 2x and * to ** 1x, dc in same st as first st, ch1, join with dc to first st. {64 sts on each side; 4 2-ch cnr sps}

R29: ch3 (stch), *32x [skip 1 st, tr in next st, tr in skipped st]**, tr in 2-ch cnr sp*, rep from * to * 2x and * to ** 1x, join with ss to 3rd ch of stch. {64 sts on each side; 4 1-st cnrs}

R30: ch3 (stch), *ch1, skip 1 st, 31x [tr between last and next sts, ch1, skip 2 sts], tr between last and next sts, ch1, skip 1 st**, (tr, ch2, tr) in next st*, rep from * to * 2x and * to ** 1x, tr in same st as first st, ch1, join with dc to 3rd ch of stch.
{34 sts, 33 1-ch sps on each side; 4 2-ch cnr sps}

R31: dc over joining dc, *33x [dc in next st, dc in 1-ch sp], dc in next st**, (dc, ch2, dc) in 2-ch cnr sp*, rep from * to * 2x and * to ** 1x, dc in same sp as first st, ch1, join with dc to first st.
{69 sts on each side; 4 2-ch cnr sps}

R32: ch3 (stch), tr over joining dc, *tr in next 69 sts**, 3tr in 2-ch cnr sp*, rep from * to * 2x and * to ** 1x, tr in same sp as first sts, join with ss to 3rd ch of stch. {69 sts on each side; 4 3-st cnrs}

R33: dc in same st as ss, *dc in next 71 sts**, (dc, ch2, dc) in next st*, rep from * to * 2x and * to ** 1x, dc in same st as first st, ch1, join with dc to first st. {73 sts on each side; 4 2-ch cnr sps}

R34: ch4 (stch), (2dtrcl, 2x [ch2, 3dtrcl]) over joining dc, *skip 3 sts, dc in next st, 11x [skip 2 sts, (2x [3dtrcl, ch2], 3dtrcl) in next st, skip 2 sts, dc in next st], skip 3 sts**, (4x [3dtrcl, ch2], 3dtrcl) in 2-ch cnr sp*, rep from * to * 2x and * to ** 1x, 2x [3dtrcl, ch2] in same sp as first sts, join with ss to top of 2dtrcl. {45 sts, 22 2-ch sps on each side; 4 (5-st & 4 2-ch sp) cnrs}

R35: ss to 2-ch sp, ch4 (stch), (2dtrcl, ch2, 3dtrcl) in same sp, skip 1 st, 2x [ch2, 3dtrcl] in 2-ch sp, *skip 2 sts, 10x [fpdc around next st, ch2, skip 2-ch sp, bpdc around next st, ch2, skip 2-ch sp, fpdc around next st, dc in next st], fpdc around next st, ch2, skip 2-ch sp, bpdc around next st, ch2, skip 2-ch sp, fpdc around next st, skip 2 sts**, 3x [(3dtrcl, ch2, 3dtrcl, ch2) in 2-ch sp, skip 1 st], (3dtrcl, ch2, 3dtrcl) in 2-ch sp*, rep from * to * 2x and * to ** 1x, 2x [(3dtrcl, ch2) in 2-ch sp], skip 1 st, (3dtrcl, ch2, 3dtrcl) in 2-ch sp, ch1, join with dc to top of 2dtrcl.
{43 sts, 22 2-ch sps on each side; 4 (8-st & 7 2-ch sp) cnrs}

R36: ch4 (stch), (2dtrcl, ch2, 3dtrcl) over joining dc, *3x [ch2, skip 1 st, 3dtrcl in 2-ch sp], skip 1 st, 10x [fp3dtrcl around cl of R34, skip (1 st & 2-ch sp), bpdc around next st, skip (2-ch sp & 1 st), fp3dtrcl around cl of R34, ch2, dc in next st, ch2], fp3dtrcl around cl of R34, skip (1 st & 2-ch sp), bpdc around next st, skip (2-ch sp & 1 st), fp3dtrcl around cl of R34, skip 1 st, 3x [3dtrcl in 2-ch sp, ch2, skip 1 st]**, (2x [3dtrcl, ch2], 3dtrcl) in 2-ch cnr sp*, rep from * to * 2x and * to ** 1x, 3dtrcl in same sp as first sts, ch2, join with ss to top of 2dtrcl.
{43 sts, 20 2-ch sps on each side; 4 (9-st & 8 2-ch sp) cnrs}

R37: ch3 (stch), tr in same st as ss, *4x [2tr in 2-ch sp, (tr in, fptr around) next st], 10x [fpdc around next 2 cl sts at the same time skipping the st between, 2dc in 2-ch sp, dc in next st, 2dc in 2-ch sp], fpdc around next 2 cl sts at the same time skipping the st between, 4x [(fptr around, tr in) next st, 2tr in 2-ch sp]**, 3tr in next st*, rep from * to * 2x and * to ** 1x, tr in same st as first sts, join with ss to 3rd ch of stch. {93 sts on each side; 4 3-st cnrs}

R38: ch3 (stch), tr in same st as ss, *tr in next 16 sts, tr3tog over next 3 sts, tr in next 57 sts, tr3tog over next 3 sts, tr in next 16 sts**, 3tr in next st*, rep from * to * 2x and * to ** 1x, tr in same st as first sts, join with ss to 3rd ch of stch. {91 sts on each side; 4 3-st cnrs}

R39: dc in same st as ss, *dc in next 17 sts, dc2tog, dc in next 55 sts, dc2tog, dc in next 17 sts**, (dc, ch2, dc) in next st*, rep from * to * 2x and * to ** 1x, dc in same st as first st, ch1, join with dc to first st. {93 sts on each side; 4 2-ch cnr sps}

R40: dc over joining dc, *3x [skip 2 sts, 7tr in next st, skip 2 sts, dc in next st], 19x [skip 2 sts, tr in next st, tr in 2nd skipped st, tr in first skipped st], 3x [dc in next st, skip 2 sts, 7tr in next st, skip 2 sts]**, dc in 2-ch cnr sp*, rep from * to * 2x and * to ** 1x, join with ss to first st. {105 sts on each side; 4 1-st cnrs}

R41: dc in same st as ss, *3x [fptr around next 7 sts, fpdc around next st], 18x [ch2, tr3tog over next 3 sts, ch2, dc between last and next sts], ch2, tr3tog over next 3 sts, ch2, 3x [fpdc around next st, fptr around next 7 sts]**, dc in next st*, rep from * to * 2x and * to ** 1x, join with ss to first st. {85 sts, 38 2-ch sps on each side; 4 1-st cnrs}

R42: fptr around cnr st of R40 below, *3x [tr in next 7 sts of R40 behind, skip 7 sts, dc in next st], ch2, skip 2-ch sp, 18x [fpdc around next st, ch2, skip (2-ch sp, 1 st & 2-ch sp)], fpdc around next st, ch2, skip 2-ch sp, 3x [dc in next st, tr in next 7 sts of R40 behind, skip 7 sts]**, fptr around cnr st of R40 below*, rep from * to * 2x and * to ** 1x, join with ss to first st. {67 sts, 20 2-ch sps on each side; 4 1-st cnrs}

R43: dc in same st as ss, *3x [2dc in next 7 sts, fptr around next st of R40 below, skip 1 st], skip 2-ch sp, 18x [fpdc around next st, 3tr in next st of R41 over 2-ch sp], fpdc around next st, skip 2-ch sp, 3x [fptr around next st of R40 below, skip 1 st, 2dc in next 7 sts]**, dc in next st*, rep from * to * 2x and * to ** 1x, join with ss to first st. {163 sts on each side; 4 1-st cnrs}

R44: ch3 (stch), tr in same st as ss, *3x [bptr around next 7 sts of R42, skip 14 sts, dc in next st], 17x [dc in next st, ch2, bptr around next st of R41 below, ch2, skip 3 sts], dc in next st, ch2, bptr around next st of R41 below, ch2, skip 3 sts, dc in next st, 3x [dc in next st, bptr around next 7 sts of R42, skip 14 sts]**, 3tr in next st*, rep from * to * 2x and * to ** 1x, tr in same st as first sts, join with ss to 3rd ch of stch. {85 sts, 36 2-ch sps on each side; 4 3-st cnrs}

R45: **This round will be very ruffled along side.** ch3 (stch), *tr in next 7 sts, tr3tog over next 3 sts, tr in next 5 sts, tr3tog over next 3 sts, tr in next 7 sts, 18x [dc in next st, ch1, skip 2-ch sp, 5tr in next st, ch1, skip 2-ch sp], dc in next st, tr in next 7 sts, tr3tog over next 3 sts, tr in next 5 sts, tr3tog over next 3 sts, tr in next 7 sts**, (tr, ch2, tr) in next st*, rep from * to * 2x and * to ** 1x, tr in same st as first st, ch1, join with dc to 3rd ch of stch. {153 sts, 36 1-ch sps on each side; 4 2-ch cnr sps}

R46: dc over joining dc, *dc in next 23 sts, 17x [tr in 1-ch sp, tr in both 1-ch sps either side of next 5 sts at the same time, tr in same 1-ch sp, tr in next st], tr in 1-ch sp, tr in both 1-ch sps either side of next 5 sts at the same time, tr in same 1-ch sp, dc in next 23 sts**, (dc, ch2, dc) in 2-ch cnr sp*, rep from * to * 2x and * to ** 1x, dc in same sp as first st, ch1, join with dc to first st. {119 sts on each side; 4 2-ch cnr sps}

R47: dc over joining dc, *dc in next 25 sts, 17x [skip next st, dc in next 3 sts], skip next st, dc in next 25 sts**, (dc, ch2, dc) in 2-ch cnr sp*, rep from * to * 2x and * to ** 1x, dc in same sp as first st, ch1, join with dc to first st. {103 sts on each side; 4 2-ch cnr sps}

R48: ch3 (stch), *tr in next 103 sts**, (tr, ch2, tr) in 2-ch cnr sp*, rep from * to * 2x and * to ** 1x, tr in same sp as first st, ch1, join with dc to 3rd ch of stch. {105 sts on each side; 4 2-ch cnr sps}

R49: dc over joining dc, *dc in next 105 sts**, (dc, ch2, dc) in 2-ch cnr sp*, rep from * to * 2x and * to ** 1x, dc in same sp as first st, ch2, join with ss to first st. Fasten off.
{107 sts on each side; 4 2-ch cnr sps}

Avalon
Granny Square Pattern

US TERMS

Begin with mc.

R1: ch1, *sc, 5dc*, rep from * to * 3x, join with ss to first st. {24 sts}

R2: ch3 (stch), *ch2, skip 2 sts, sc in next st, ch2, skip 2 sts**, dc in next st*, rep from * to * 2x and * to ** 1x, join with ss to 3rd ch of stch. {8 sts, 8 2-ch sps}

R3: sc in same st as ss, *3sc in 2-ch sp**, sc in next st*, rep from * to * 6x and * to ** 1x, join with ss to first st. {32 sts}

R4: ch3 (stch), dc in same st as ss, *dc in next 3 sts**, 2dc in next st*, rep from * to * 6x and * to ** 1x, join with ss to 3rd ch of stch. {40 sts}

R5: sc in same st as ss, sc in next 39 sts, join with ss to first st. {40 sts}

R6: sc in same st as ss, *ch1, fphtr around R4 st below next st, ch1, skip 1 st**, sc in next st*, rep from * to * 18x and * to ** 1x, join with ss to first st. {40 sts, 40 1-ch sps}

R7: ch3 (stch), *dc in 1-ch sp, fphtr around next st, dc in 1-ch sp**, dc in next st*, rep from * to * 18x and * to ** 1x, join with ss to 3rd ch of stch. {80 sts}

R8: sc in same st as ss, *skip 1 st, (fphtr around, dc in, fphtr around) next st, skip 1 st**, sc in next st*, rep from * to * 18x and * to ** 1x, join with ss to first st. {80 sts}

R9: **This round will be very ruffled.** ch3 (stch), *(fpdc around, dc in) next st, ch1, 5dc in next st, ch1, (dc in, fpdc around) next st**, dc in next st*, rep from * to * 18x and * to ** 1x, join with ss to 3rd ch of stch. {200 sts, 40 1-ch sps}

R10: ch1, fpsc around 2 fp sts at the same time skipping st ss'd into, *sc in next st, sc in both 1-ch sps either side of next 5 sts at the same time, sc in next st**, fpsc around next 2 fp sts at the same time skipping st between*, rep from * to * 18x and * to ** 1x, join with ss to first st. {80 sts}

R11: sc in same st as ss, sc in next 79 sts, join with ss to first st. {80 sts}

R12: sc in same st as ss, *ch2, skip 1 st**, sc in next st*, rep from * to * 38x and * to ** 1x, join with ss to first st. {40 sts, 40 2-ch sps}

R13: fpss around st ss'd into, ch3 (stch), ch2, fphtr around same st as ss, *2dc in 2-ch sp**, (fphtr around, ch2, fphtr around) next st*, rep from * to * 38x and * to ** 1x, join with ss to 3rd ch of stch. {160 sts, 40 2-ch sps}

R14: ch3 (stch), *5dc in 2-ch sp, (dc in, fpdc around) next st, skip 3 sts, sc in 2-ch sp, skip 3 sts**, (fpdc around, dc in) next st*, rep from * to * 18x and * to ** 1x, fpdc around next st, join with ss to 3rd ch of stch. {200 sts}

R15: *sc in next 2 sts, 3dc in next st, sc in next 2 sts, skip 1 st, fpsc around next 2 fp sts at the same time skipping st between**, skip 1 st*, rep from * to * 18x and * to ** 1x, do not join. {160 sts}

R16: sc in last st of R15, *ch5, skip 7 sts**, sc in next st*, rep from * to * 18x and * to ** 1x, join with ss to first st. {20 sts, 20 5-ch sps}

R17: ch3 (stch), 3dc in same st as ss, *sc in 5-ch sp**, 7dc in next st*, rep from * to * 18x and * to ** 1x, 3dc in same st as first sts, join with ss to 3rd ch of stch. {160 sts}

R18: ch3 (stch), dc in same st as ss, *2dc in next 3 sts, skip 4 sts, sc in next st, skip 4 sts, 2dc in next 3 sts**, (2dc, ch2, 2dc) in next st*, rep from * to * 8x and * to ** 1x, 2dc in same st as first sts, ch1, join with sc to 3rd ch of stch. {170 sts, 10 2-ch sps}

R19: ch2 (stch), *hdc in next 8 sts, ss in next st, hdc in next 8 sts**, hdc in 2-ch sp*, rep from * to * 8x and * to ** 1x, join with inv join to first true st. {180 sts}

R20: Attach with stdg dc2tog in lbv of the sts either side of any ss, *hdc in lbv of next 4 sts, sc in lbv of next 7 sts, hdc in lbv of next 4 sts**, dc2tog in lbv of next 3 sts skipping the middle st*, rep from * to * 8x and * to ** 1x, join with ss to first st. {160 sts}

R21: ch3 (stch), *dc in next 2 sts, hdc in next 3 sts, sc in next 5 sts, hdc in next 3 sts, dc in next 2 sts**, 2dc in next st*, rep from * to * 8x and * to ** 1x, dc in same st as first st, join with ss to 3rd ch of stch. {170 sts}

R22: sc in same st as ss, sc in next 7 sts, *2sc in next st**, sc in next 16 sts*, rep from * to * 8x and * to ** 1x, sc in next 8 sts, join with ss to first st. {180 sts}

R23: ch4, (2trcl, ch2, 3trcl) in same st as ss, *ch2, skip 1 st, 3trcl in next st, skip 3 sts, sc in next 34 sts, skip 3 sts, 3trcl in next st, ch2, skip 1 st**, (2x [3trcl, ch2], 3trcl) in next st*, rep from * to * 2x and * to ** 1x, 3trcl in same st as first sts, ch2, join with ss to top of 2trcl. {34 sts on each side; 4 (5-st & 4 2-ch sp) cnrs}

R24: ss to 2-ch sp, ch4 (stch), (2trcl, ch2, 3trcl) in same sp, skip 1 st, 2x [ch2, 3trcl] in 2-ch sp, *skip 4 sts, sc in next 28 sts, skip 4 sts**, 3x [(3trcl, ch2, 3trcl, ch2) in 2-ch sp, skip 1 st], (3trcl, ch2, 3trcl) in 2-ch sp*, rep from * to * 2x and * to ** 1x, 2x [(3trcl, ch2) in 2-ch sp], skip 1 st, (3trcl, ch2, 3trcl) in 2-ch sp, skip 1 st, ch1, join with sc to top of 2trcl. {28 sts on each side; 4 (8-st & 7 2-ch sp) cnrs}

R25: ch4 (stch), (2trcl, ch2, 3trcl) over joining sc, *3x [ch2, skip 1 st, 3trcl] in 2-ch sp, skip 3 sts, sc in next 24 sts, skip 3 sts, 3x [3trcl in 2-ch sp, ch2, skip 1 st]**, (2x [3trcl, ch2], 3trcl) in 2-ch cnr sp*, rep from * to * 2x and * to ** 1x, 3trcl in same sp as first sts, ch2, join with ss to top of 2trcl. {24 sts on each side; 4 (9-st & 8 2-ch sp) cnrs}

R26: sc in same st as ss, *4x [3sc in 2-ch sp, fpsc around next st], sc between last and next sts, sc in next 24 sts, sc between last and next sts, 4x [fpsc around next st, 3sc in 2-ch sp]**, (sc, ch2, sc) in next st*, rep from * to * 2x and * to ** 1x, sc in same st as first st, ch1, join with sc to first st. {60 sts on each side; 4 2-ch cnr sps}

R27: ch3 (stch), dc over joining sc, *dc in next 60 sts**, 3dc in 2-ch cnr sp*, rep from * to * 2x and * to ** 1x, dc in same sp as first sts, join with ss to 3rd ch of stch.
{60 sts on each side; 4 3-st cnrs}

R28: sc in same st as ss, *sc in next 62 sts**, (sc, ch2, sc) in next st*, rep from * to * 2x and * to ** 1x, sc in same st as first st, ch1, join with sc to first st. {64 sts on each side; 4 2-ch cnr sps}

R29: ch3 (stch), *32x [skip 1 st, dc in next st, dc in skipped st]**, dc in 2-ch cnr sp*, rep from * to * 2x and * to ** 1x, join with ss to 3rd ch of stch. {64 sts on each side; 4 1-st cnrs}

R30: ch3 (stch), *ch1, skip 1 st, 31x [dc between last and next sts, ch1, skip 2 sts], dc between last and next sts, ch1, skip 1 st**, (dc, ch2, dc) in next st*, rep from * to * 2x and * to ** 1x, dc in same st as first st, ch1, join with sc to 3rd ch of stch.
{34 sts, 33 1-ch sps on each side; 4 2-ch cnr sps}

R31: sc over joining sc, *33x [sc in next st, sc in 1-ch sp], sc in next st**, (sc, ch2, sc) in 2-ch cnr sp*, rep from * to * 2x and * to ** 1x, sc in same sp as first st, ch1, join with sc to first st.
{69 sts on each side; 4 2-ch cnr sps}

R32: ch3 (stch), dc over joining sc, *dc in next 69 sts**, 3dc in 2-ch cnr sp*, rep from * to * 2x and * to ** 1x, dc in same sp as first sts, join with ss to 3rd ch of stch.
{69 sts on each side; 4 3-st cnrs}

R33: sc in same st as ss, *sc in next 71 sts**, (sc, ch2, sc) in next st*, rep from * to * 2x and * to ** 1x, sc in same st as first st, ch1, join with sc to first st. {73 sts on each side; 4 2-ch cnr sps}

R34: ch4 (stch), (2trcl, 2x [ch2, 3trcl]) over joining sc, *skip 3 sts, sc in next st, 11x [skip 2 sts, (2x [3trcl, ch2], 3trcl) in next st, skip 2 sts, sc in next st], skip 3 sts**, (4x [3trcl, ch2], 3trcl) in 2-ch cnr sp*, rep from * to * 2x and * to ** 1x, 2x [3trcl, ch2] in same sp as first sts, join with ss to top of 2trcl. {45 sts, 22 2-ch sps on each side; 4 (5-st & 4 2-ch sp) cnrs}

R35: ss to 2-ch sp, ch4 (stch), (2trcl, ch2, 3trcl) in same sp, skip 1 st, 2x [ch2, 3trcl] in 2-ch sp, *skip 2 sts, 10x [fpsc around next st, ch2, skip 2-ch sp, bpsc around next st, ch2, skip 2-ch sp, fpsc around next st, sc in next st], fpsc around next st, ch2, skip 2-ch sp, bpsc around next st, ch2, skip 2-ch sp, fpsc around next st, skip 2 sts**, 3x [(3trcl, ch2, 3trcl, ch2) in 2-ch sp, skip 1 st], (3trcl, ch2, 3trcl) in 2-ch sp*, rep from * to * 2x and * to ** 1x, 2x [(3trcl, ch2) in 2-ch sp], skip 1 st, (3trcl, ch2, 3trcl) in 2-ch sp, ch1, join with sc to top of 2trcl.
{43 sts, 22 2-ch sps on each side; 4 (8-st & 7 2-ch sp) cnrs}

R36: ch4 (stch), (2trcl, ch2, 3trcl) over joining sc, *3x [ch2, skip 1 st, 3trcl in 2-ch sp], skip 1 st, 10x [fp3trcl around cl of R34, skip (1 st & 2-ch sp), bpsc around next st, skip (2-ch sp & 1 st), fp3trcl around cl of R34, ch2, sc in next st, ch2], fp3trcl around cl of R34, skip (1 st & 2-ch sp), bpsc around next st, skip (2-ch sp & 1 st), fp3trcl around cl of R34, skip 1 st, 3x [3trcl in 2-ch sp, ch2, skip 1 st]**, (2x [3trcl, ch2], 3trcl) in 2-ch cnr sp*, rep from * to * 2x and * to ** 1x, 3trcl in same sp as first sts, ch2, join with ss to top of 2trcl.
{43 sts, 20 2-ch sps on each side; 4 (9-st & 8 2-ch sp) cnrs}

R37: ch3 (stch), dc in same st as ss, *4x [2dc in 2-ch sp, (dc in, fpdc around) next st], 10x [fpsc around next 2 cl sts at the same time skipping the st between, 2sc in 2-ch sp, sc in next st, 2sc in 2-ch sp], fpsc around next 2 cl sts at the same time skipping the st between, 4x [(fpdc around, dc in) next st, 2dc in 2-ch sp]**, 3dc in next st*, rep from * to * 2x and * to ** 1x, dc in same st as first sts, join with ss to 3rd ch of stch. {93 sts on each side; 4 3-st cnrs}

R38: ch3 (stch), dc in same st as ss, *dc in next 16 sts, dc3tog over next 3 sts, dc in next 57 sts, dc3tog over next 3 sts, dc in next 16 sts**, 3dc in next st*, rep from * to * 2x and * to ** 1x, dc in same st as first sts, join with ss to 3rd ch of stch. {91 sts on each side; 4 3-st cnrs}

R39: sc in same st as ss, *sc in next 17 sts, sc2tog, sc in next 55 sts, sc2tog, sc in next 17 sts**, (sc, ch2, sc) in next st*, rep from * to * 2x and * to ** 1x, sc in same st as first st, ch1, join with sc to first st. {93 sts on each side; 4 2-ch cnr sps}

R40: sc over joining sc, *3x [skip 2 sts, 7dc in next st, skip 2 sts, sc in next st], 19x [skip 2 sts, dc in next st, dc in 2nd skipped st, dc in first skipped st], 3x [sc in next st, skip 2 sts, 7dc in next st, skip 2 sts]**, sc in 2-ch cnr sp*, rep from * to * 2x and * to ** 1x, join with ss to first st. {105 sts on each side; 4 1-st cnrs}

R41: sc in same st as ss, *3x [fpdc around next 7 sts, fpsc around next st], 18x [ch2, dc3tog over next 3 sts, ch2, sc between last and next sts], ch2, dc3tog over next 3 sts, ch2, 3x [fpsc around next st, fpdc around next 7 sts]**, sc in next st*, rep from * to * 2x and * to ** 1x, join with ss to first st. {85 sts, 38 2-ch sps on each side; 4 1-st cnrs}

R42: fpdc around cnr st of R40 below, *3x [dc in next 7 sts of R40 behind, skip 7 sts, sc in next st], ch2, skip 2-ch sp, 18x [fpsc around next st, ch2, skip (2-ch sp, 1 st & 2-ch sp)], fpsc around next st, ch2, skip 2-ch sp, 3x [sc in next st, dc in next 7 sts of R40 behind, skip 7 sts]**, fpdc around cnr st of R40 below*, rep from * to * 2x and * to ** 1x, join with ss to first st. {67 sts, 20 2-ch sps on each side; 4 1-st cnrs}

R43: sc in same st as ss, *3x [2sc in next 7 sts, fpdc around next st of R40 below, skip 1 st], skip 2-ch sp, 18x [fpsc around next st, 3dc in next st of R41 over 2-ch sp], fpsc around next st, skip 2-ch sp, 3x [fpdc around next st of R40 below, skip 1 st, 2sc in next 7 sts]**, sc in next st*, rep from * to * 2x and * to ** 1x, join with ss to first st. {163 sts on each side; 4 1-st cnrs}

R44: ch3 (stch), dc in same st as ss, *3x [bpdc around next 7 sts of R42, skip 14 sts, sc in next st], 17x [sc in next st, ch2, bpdc around next st of R41 below, ch2, skip 3 sts], sc in next st, ch2, bpdc around next st of R41 below, ch2, skip 3 sts, sc in next st, 3x [sc in next st, bpdc around next 7 sts of R42, skip 14 sts]**, 3dc in next st*, rep from * to * 2x and * to ** 1x, dc in same st as first sts, join with ss to 3rd ch of stch. {85 sts, 36 2-ch sps on each side; 4 3-st cnrs}

R45: **This round will be very ruffled along side.** ch3 (stch), *dc in next 7 sts, dc3tog over next 3 sts, dc in next 5 sts, dc3tog over next 3 sts, dc in next 7 sts, 18x [sc in next st, ch1, skip 2-ch sp, 5dc in next st, ch1, skip 2-ch sp], sc in next st, dc in next 7 sts, dc3tog over next 3 sts, dc in next 5 sts, dc3tog over next 3 sts, dc in next 7 sts**, (dc, ch2, dc) in next st*, rep from * to * 2x and * to ** 1x, dc in same st as first st, ch1, join with sc to 3rd ch of stch. {153 sts, 36 1-ch sps on each side; 4 2-ch cnr sps}

R46: sc over joining sc, *sc in next 23 sts, 17x [dc in 1-ch sp, dc in both 1-ch sps either side of next 5 sts at the same time, dc in same 1-ch sp, dc in next st], dc in 1-ch sp, dc in both 1-ch sps either side of next 5 sts at the same time, dc in same 1-ch sp, sc in next 23 sts**, (sc, ch2, sc) in 2-ch cnr sp*, rep from * to * 2x and * to ** 1x, sc in same sp as first st, ch1, join with sc to first st. {119 sts on each side; 4 2-ch cnr sps}

R47: sc over joining sc, *sc in next 25 sts, 17x [skip next st, sc in next 3 sts], skip next st, sc in next 25 sts**, (sc, ch2, sc) in 2-ch cnr sp*, rep from * to * 2x and * to ** 1x, sc in same sp as first st, ch1, join with sc to first st. {103 sts on each side; 4 2-ch cnr sps}

R48: ch3 (stch), *dc in next 103 sts**, (dc, ch2, dc) in 2-ch cnr sp*, rep from * to * 2x and * to ** 1x, dc in same sp as first st, ch1, join with sc to 3rd ch of stch.
{105 sts on each side; 4 2-ch cnr sps}

R49: sc over joining sc, *sc in next 105 sts**, (sc, ch2, sc) in 2-ch cnr sp*, rep from * to * 2x and * to ** 1x, sc in same sp as first st, ch2, join with ss to first st. Fasten off.
{107 sts on each side; 4 2-ch cnr sps}

Joining
Caltha Squares

Now it's time to leave the misty isle of Avalon and travel into the real world.

Make 24 of the Caltha pattern. Join them into two strips of five squares and two strips of seven squares. Attach the 5-square strips to opposite sides of the centre piece, then attach the two 7-square strips to the other edges.

✳ *Nimue's Counsel*

Visit the end of the Caltha Help on page 89 for advice on how to join the Caltha squares into strips as you go.

Join squares as follows:

Hold squares right sides together, attach joining yarn with a standing double crochet (UK)/single crochet (US) to both 2-chain corner spaces of each square at the same time. Work a stitch into both loops of both squares all the way along, end with a stitch in both 2-chain corner spaces. Fasten off.

When attaching strips to centre piece, use each stitch, 2-chain space and join with each stitch and corner chain spaces of the centre square.

stitch in 2-chain space — stitch in join — stitch in 2-chain space

Caltha
Granny Square Pattern

UK TERMS

Begin with mc.

R1: ch4 (stch), 2dtrcl, *ch2**, 3dtrcl*, rep from * to * 6x and * to ** 1x, join with ss to top of 2dtrcl. {8 sts, 8 2-ch sps}

R2: dc in same st as ss, *3dc in 2-ch sp**, 2dc in next st*, rep from * to * 6x and * to ** 1x, dc in same st as first st, join with ss to first st. {40 sts}

R3: ch3 (stch), *4x [skip 1 st, tr in next st, tr in skipped st], tr in next st**, ch2, tr in next st*, rep from * to * 2x and * to ** 1x, ch1, join with dc to 3rd ch of stch.
{10 sts on each side; 4 2-ch cnr sps}

R4: ch3 (stch), *tr in next st, ch1, skip 1 st, 3x [tr between last and next sts, ch1, skip 2 sts], tr between last & next sts, ch1, skip 1 st, tr in next st**, (tr, ch2, tr) in 2-ch cnr sp*, rep from * to * 2x and * to ** 1x, tr in same sp as first st, ch1, join with dc to 3rd ch of stch.
{8 sts, 5 1-ch sps on each side; 4 2-ch cnr sps}

R5: dc over joining dc, *dc in next 2 sts, 4x [dc in 1-ch sp, dc in next st], dc in 1-ch sp, dc in next 2 sts**, (dc, ch2, dc) in 2-ch cnr sp*, rep from * to * 2x and * to ** 1x, dc in same sp as first st, ch1, join with dc to first st. {15 sts on each side; 4 2-ch cnr sps}

R6: ch3 (stch), *hdtr in next 15 sts**, (hdtr, ch2, hdtr) in 2-ch cnr sp*, rep from * to * 2x and * to ** 1x, hdtr in same sp as first st, ch1, join with dc to 3rd ch of stch.
{17 sts on each side; 4 2-ch cnr sps}

R7: dc over joining dc, *dc in next 17 sts**, (dc, ch2, dc) in 2-ch cnr sp*, rep from * to * 2x and * to ** 1x, dc in same sp as first st, ch2, join with ss to first st. Fasten off.
{19 sts on each side; 4 2-ch cnr sps}

Caltha
Granny Square Pattern

US TERMS

Begin with mc.

R1: ch4 (stch), 2trcl, *ch2**, 3trcl*, rep from * to * 6x and * to ** 1x, join with ss to top of 2trcl. {8 sts, 8 2-ch sps}

R2: sc in same st as ss, *3sc in 2-ch sp**, 2sc in next st*, rep from * to * 6x and * to ** 1x, sc in same st as first st, join with ss to first st. {40 sts}

R3: ch3 (stch), *4x [skip 1 st, dc in next st, dc in skipped st], dc in next st**, ch2, dc in next st*, rep from * to * 2x and * to ** 1x, ch1, join with sc to 3rd ch of stch. {10 sts on each side; 4 2-ch cnr sps}

R4: ch3 (stch), *dc in next st, ch1, skip 1 st, 3x [dc between last and next sts, ch1, skip 2 sts], dc between last & next sts, ch1, skip 1 st, dc in next st**, (dc, ch2, dc) in 2-ch cnr sp*, rep from * to * 2x and * to ** 1x, dc in same sp as first st, ch1, join with sc to 3rd ch of stch. {8 sts, 5 1-ch sps on each side; 4 2-ch cnr sps}

R5: sc over joining sc, *sc in next 2 sts, 4x [sc in 1-ch sp, sc in next st], sc in 1-ch sp, sc in next 2 sts**, (sc, ch2, sc) in 2-ch cnr sp*, rep from * to * 2x and * to ** 1x, sc in same sp as first st, ch1, join with sc to first st. {15 sts on each side; 4 2-ch cnr sps}

R6: ch3 (stch), *htr in next 15 sts**, (htr, ch2, htr) in 2-ch cnr sp*, rep from * to * 2x and * to ** 1x, htr in same sp as first st, ch1, join with sc to 3rd ch of stch. {17 sts on each side; 4 2-ch cnr sps}

R7: sc over joining sc, *sc in next 17 sts**, (sc, ch2, sc) in 2-ch cnr sp*, rep from * to * 2x and * to ** 1x, sc in same sp as first st, ch2, join with ss to first st. Fasten off. {19 sts on each side; 4 2-ch cnr sps}

Nimue
Blanket Pattern

UK TERMS

R50: Attach with stdg dc to any 2-ch cnr sp, *6x [dc in next 19 sts, dc in 2-ch sp, dc in join, dc in 2-ch sp], dc in next 19 sts**, (dc, ch2, dc) in 2-ch cnr sp*, rep from * to * 2x and * to ** 1x, dc in same sp as first st, ch1, join with dc to first st. {153 sts on each side; 4 2-ch cnr sps}

R51: ch3 (stch), *tr in next 153 sts**, (tr, ch2, tr) in 2-ch cnr sp*, rep from * to * 2x and * to ** 1x, tr in same sp as first st, ch1, join with dc to 3rd ch of stch. {155 sts on each side; 4 2-ch cnr sps}

R52: dc over joining dc, *dc in next 155 sts**, (dc, ch2, dc) in 2-ch cnr sp*, rep from * to * 2x and * to ** 1x, dc in same sp as first st, ch1, join with dc to first st.
{157 sts on each side; 4 2-ch cnr sps}

R53: dc over joining dc, *skip 3 sts, 25x [7tr in next st, skip 2 sts, dc in next st, skip 2 sts], 7tr in next st, skip 3 sts**, dc in 2-ch cnr sp*, rep from * to * 2x and * to ** 1x, join with ss to first st. {207 sts on each side; 4 1-st cnrs}

R54: dc in same st as ss, *25x [fptr around next 7 sts, fpdc around next st], fptr around next 7 sts**, dc in next st*, rep from * to * 2x and * to ** 1x, join with ss to first st.
{207 sts on each side; 4 1-st cnrs}

R55: *Note: the stitches along the side are all worked into R53 sts behind R54.* ch3 (stch), tr in same st as ss, *tr in next st of R53 behind, 25x [htr in next st of R53 behind, dc in next 3 sts of R53 behind, htr in next st of R53 behind, tr3tog over next 3 sts of R53 behind], htr in next st of R53 behind, dc in next 3 sts of R53 behind, htr in next st of R53 behind, tr in next st of R53 behind**, skip 207 sts, (2tr, ch2, 2tr) in next st*, rep from * to * 2x and * to ** 1x, 2tr in same st as first sts, ch1, join with dc to 3rd ch of stch.
{161 sts on each side; 4 2-ch cnr sps}

R56: dc over joining dc, *dc in next 5 sts, 24x [dc in lbv of 4th st of the 7-st group of R54 & next st at the same time, dc in next 2 sts, fpdc around next st, dc in next 2 sts], dc in lbv of 4th st of the 7-st group of R54 & next st at the same time, dc in next 5 sts**, (dc, ch2, dc) in 2-ch cnr sp*, rep from * to * 2x and * to ** 1x, dc in same sp as first st, ch1, join with dc to first st.
{163 sts on each side; 4 2-ch cnr sps}

R57: ch3 (stch), tr over joining dc, *skip 1 st, 54x [skip 2 sts, tr in next st, tr in 2nd skipped st, tr in first skipped st]**, (2tr, ch2, 2tr) in 2-ch cnr sp*, rep from * to * 2x and * to ** 1x, 2tr in same sp as first sts, ch1, join with dc to 3rd ch of stch. {166 sts on each side; 4 2-ch cnr sps}

R58: dc over joining dc, *dc in next 2 sts, 54x [dc between last and next sts, dc in next 3 sts], dc between last and next sts, dc in next 2 sts**, (dc, ch2, dc) in 2-ch cnr sp*, rep from * to * 2x and * to ** 1x, dc in same sp as first st, ch1, join with dc to first st. {223 sts on each side; 4 2-ch cnr sps}

R59: ch3 (stch), tr over joining dc, *tr in next st, fpdtr around next 2 sts of R57, skip 2 sts, 54x [htr in next st, fpdtr3tog around and over next 3 sts of R57, skip 3 sts], htr in next st, fpdtr around next 2 sts of R57, skip 2 sts, tr in next st**, 3tr in 2-ch cnr sp*, rep from * to * 2x and * to ** 1x, tr in same sp as first sts, join with ss to 3rd ch of stch. {115 sts on each side; 4 3-st cnrs}

R60: ch3 (stch), tr in same st as ss, *fptr around next 4 sts, 54x [tr in next st, (tr in, fptr around) next st], tr in next st, fptr around next 4 sts**, 3tr in next st*, rep from * to * 2x and * to ** 1x, tr in same st as first sts, join with ss to 3rd ch of stch. {171 sts on each side; 4 3-st cnrs}

R61: ch3 (stch), tr in same st as ss, *fptr around next 5 sts, skip 1 st, dc in next st, 26x [skip 2 sts, 7tr in next st, skip 2 sts, dc in next st], skip 2 sts, 7tr in next st, skip 1 st, dc in next st, fptr around next 5 sts**, 3tr in next st*, rep from * to * 2x and * to ** 1x, tr in same st as first sts, join with ss to 3rd ch of stch. {227 sts on each side; 4 3-st cnrs}

R62: ch3 (stch), tr in same st as ss, *fptr around next 6 sts, 27x [fpdc around next st, fptr around next 7 sts], fpdc around next st, fptr around next 6 sts**, 3tr in next st*, rep from * to * 2x and * to ** 1x, tr in same st as first sts, join with ss to 3rd ch of stch. {229 sts on each side; 4 3-st cnrs}

R63: **Note: the stitches along the side are all worked into R61 sts behind R62.** ch3 (stch), tr in same st as ss, *fptr around next 7 sts, tr2tog over next 2 sts of R61 behind, 26x [htr in next st of R61 behind, dc in next 3 sts of R61 behind, htr in next st of R61 behind, tr3tog over next 3 sts of R61 behind], htr in next st of R61 behind, dc in next 3 sts of R61 behind, htr in next st of R61 behind, tr2tog over next 2 sts of R61 behind, fptr around next 7 sts**, 3tr in next st*, rep from * to * 2x and * to ** 1x, tr in same st as first sts, join with ss to 3rd ch of stch. {177 sts on each side; 4 3-st cnrs}

R64: dc in same st as ss, *dc in next 11 sts, 26x [dc in lbv of 4th st of the 7-st group of R62 & next st at the same time, dc in next 2 sts, 2dc in next st, dc in next 2 sts], dc in lbv of 4th st of the 7-st group of R62 & next st at the same time, dc in next 11 sts**, (dc, ch2, dc), in next st*, rep from * to * 2x and * to ** 1x, dc in same st as first st, ch1, join with dc to first st. {207 sts on each side; 4 2-ch cnr sps}

R65: ch3 (stch), *tr in next 207 sts**, (tr, ch2, tr) in 2-ch cnr sp*, rep from * to * 2x and * to ** 1x, tr in same sp as first st, ch1, join with dc to 3rd ch of stch. {209 sts on each side; 4 2-ch cnr sps}

R66: dc over joining dc, *dc in next 209 sts**, (dc, ch2, dc), in next st*, rep from * to * 2x and * to ** 1x, dc in same st as first st, ch1, join with dc to first st. {211 sts on each side; 4 2-ch cnr sps}

R67: ch3 (stch), *tr in next 211 sts**, (tr, ch2, tr) in 2-ch cnr sp*, rep from * to * 2x and * to ** 1x, tr in same sp as first st, ch1, join with dc to 3rd ch of stch. {213 sts on each side; 4 2-ch cnr sps}

R68: ch3 (stch), *106x [fptr around next st, htr in next st], fptr around next st**, (tr, ch2, tr) in 2-ch cnr sp*, rep from * to * 2x and * to ** 1x, tr in same sp as first st, ch1, join with dc to 3rd ch of stch. {215 sts on each side; 4 2-ch cnr sps}

R69: ch4 (stch), (2dtrcl, ch2, 3dtrcl) over joining dc, *skip 1 st, fptr around next st, 35x [tr in next 2 sts, starting in same st as last st fpdtr3tog over next 5 sts skipping the 2nd and 4th sts, tr in same st as last st], tr in next st, fptr around next st, skip 1 st**, (2x [3dtrcl, ch2], 3dtrcl) in 2-ch cnr sp*, rep from * to * 2x and * to ** 1x, 3dtrcl in same sp as first sts, ch2, join with ss to top of 2dtrcl. {143 sts on each side; 4 (3-st & 2 2-ch sp) cnrs}

R70: dc in same st as ss, *2dc in 2-ch sp, 2dc in next st, fptr around next st, tr in next 2 sts, 34x [ch2, skip 1 st, tr in next 3 sts], ch2, skip 1 st, tr in next 2 sts, fptr around next st, 2dc in next st, 2dc in 2-ch sp**, (dc, ch2, dc) next st*, rep from * to * 2x and * to ** 1x, dc in same st as first st, ch1, join with dc to first st. {118 sts, 35 2-ch sps on each side; 4 2-ch cnr sps}

R71: dc over joining dc, *dc in next 5 sts, fptr around next st, 35x [dc in next st, (2x [dtr, ch2]) in cl of R69 below, fpdtr around same st, skip (1 st, 2-ch sp & 1 st)], dc in next st, fptr around next st, dc in next 5 sts**, (dc, ch2, dc) in 2-ch cnr sp*, rep from * to * 2x and * to ** 1x, dc in same sp as first st, ch1, join with dc to first st. {155 sts on each side; 4 2-ch cnr sps}

R72: ch3 (stch), *tr in next 6 sts, fptr around next st, 35x [tr in next st, hdtr in skipped st of R70 behind, 2hdtr in 2-ch sp of R70 behind, hdtr in next skipped st of R70 behind, skip (2x [1 st, ch2] & 1 st)], tr in next st, fptr around next st, tr in next 6 sts**, (tr, ch2, tr) in 2-ch cnr sp*, rep from * to * 2x and * to ** 1x, tr in same sp as first st, ch1, join with dc to 3rd ch of stch. {192 sts on each side; 4 2-ch cnr sps}

R73: dc over joining dc, *dc in next 7 sts, fptr around next st, dc in next 3 sts, 34x [dc in lbv of middle dtr of R71 in front, dc in next 5 sts], dc in lbv of middle dtr of R71 in front, dc in next 3 sts, fptr around next st, dc in next 7 sts**, (dc, ch2, dc) in 2-ch cnr sp*, rep from * to * 2x and * to ** 1x, dc in same sp as first st, ch1, join with dc to first st. {229 sts on each side; 4 2-ch cnr sps}

R74: dc over joining dc, *dc2tog over next 2 sts, dc in next 10 sts, 34x [dc2tog over next 2 sts, dc in next 4 sts], dc2tog over next 2 sts, dc in next 11 sts**, (dc, ch2, dc) in 2-ch cnr sp*, rep from * to * 2x and * to ** 1x, dc in same sp as first st, ch1, join with dc to first st. {195 sts on each side; 4 2-ch cnr sps}

R75: ch3 (stch), *tr in next 195 sts**, (tr, ch2, tr) in 2-ch cnr sp*, rep from * to * 2x and * to ** 1x, tr in same sp as first st, ch1, join with dc to 3rd ch of stch. {197 sts on each side; 4 2-ch cnr sps}

R76: dc over joining dc, *dc in next 197 sts**, (dc, ch2, dc) in 2-ch cnr sp*, rep from * to * 2x and * to ** 1x, dc in same sp as first st, ch1, join with dc to first st. {199 sts on each side; 4 2-ch cnr sps}

R77: ch3 (stch), tr over joining dc, *66x [ch1, skip 1 st, tr in next 2 sts], ch1, skip 1 st**, (2tr, ch2, 2tr) in 2-ch cnr sp*, rep from * to * 2x and * to ** 1x, 2tr in same sp as first sts, ch1, join with dc to 3rd ch of stch. {136 sts, 67 1-ch sps on each side; 4 2-ch cnr sps}

R78: ch3 (stch), *67x [fptr around next 2 sts, ch1, skip 1-ch sp], fptr around next 2 sts**, (tr, ch2, tr) in 2-ch cnr sp*, rep from * to * 2x and * to ** 1x, tr in same sp as first st, ch1, join with dc to 3rd ch of stch. {138 sts, 67 1-ch sps on each side; 4 2-ch cnr sps}

R79: ch3 (stch), *fptr around next 3 sts, 66x [ch1, skip 1-ch sp, fptr around next 2 sts], ch1, skip 1-ch sp, fptr around next 3 sts**, (tr, ch2, tr) in 2-ch cnr sp*, rep from * to * 2x and * to ** 1x, tr in same sp as first st, ch1, join with dc to 3rd ch of stch.
{140 sts, 67 1-ch sps on each side; 4 2-ch cnr sps}

R80: ch3 (stch), *fptr around next 4 sts, 66x [ch1, skip 1-ch sp, fptr around next 2 sts], ch1, skip 1-ch sp, fptr around next 4 sts**, (tr, ch2, tr) in 2-ch cnr sp*, rep from * to * 2x and * to ** 1x, tr in same sp as first st, ch1, join with dc to 3rd ch of stch.
{142 sts, 67 1-ch sps on each side; 4 2-ch cnr sps}

R81: ch3 (stch), *tr in next st, 2x [ch1, tr2tog over next 2 sts], skip 1-ch sp, 66x [ch2, tr3tog over next 2 sts and 1-ch sp], ch2, 2x [tr2tog over next 2 sts, ch1], tr in next st**, (tr, ch2, tr) in 2-ch cnr sp*, rep from * to * 2x and * to ** 1x, tr in same sp as first st, ch1, join with dc to 3rd ch of stch. {74 sts, 67 2-ch sps, 4 1-ch sps on each side; 4 2-ch cnr sps}

R82: dc over joining dc, *dc in next 2 sts, 2x [dc in 1-ch sp, dc in next st], 66x [2dc in 2-ch sp, dc in next st], 2dc in 2-ch sp, 2x [dc in next st, dc in 1-ch sp], dc in next 2 sts**, (dc, ch2, dc) in 2-ch cnr sp*, rep from * to * 2x and * to ** 1x, dc in same sp as first st, ch2, join with ss to first st. Fasten off. {214 sts on each side; 4 2-ch cnr sps}

Nimue
Blanket Pattern

US TERMS

R50: Attach with stdg sc to any 2-ch cnr sp, *6x [sc in next 19 sts, sc in 2-ch sp, sc in join, sc in 2-ch sp], sc in next 19 sts**, (sc, ch2, sc) in 2-ch cnr sp*, rep from * to * 2x and * to ** 1x, sc in same sp as first st, ch1, join with sc to first st. {153 sts on each side; 4 2-ch cnr sps}

R51: ch3 (stch), *dc in next 153 sts**, (dc, ch2, dc) in 2-ch cnr sp*, rep from * to * 2x and * to ** 1x, dc in same sp as first st, ch1, join with sc to 3rd ch of stch.
{155 sts on each side; 4 2-ch cnr sps}

R52: sc over joining sc, *sc in next 155 sts**, (sc, ch2, sc) in 2-ch cnr sp*, rep from * to * 2x and * to ** 1x, sc in same sp as first st, ch1, join with sc to first st. {157 sts on each side; 4 2-ch cnr sps}

R53: sc over joining sc, *skip 3 sts, 25x [7dc in next st, skip 2 sts, sc in next st, skip 2 sts], 7dc in next st, skip 3 sts**, sc in 2-ch cnr sp*, rep from * to * 2x and * to ** 1x, join with ss to first st.
{207 sts on each side; 4 1-st cnrs}

R54: sc in same st as ss, *25x [fpdc around next 7 sts, fpsc around next st], fpdc around next 7 sts**, sc in next st*, rep from * to * 2x and * to ** 1x, join with ss to first st.
{207 sts on each side; 4 1-st cnrs}

R55: **Note: the stitches along the side are all worked into R53 sts behind R54.** ch3 (stch), dc in same st as ss, *dc in next st of R53 behind, 25x [hdc in next st of R53 behind, sc in next 3 sts of R53 behind, hdc in next st of R53 behind, dc3tog over next 3 sts of R53 behind], hdc in next st of R53 behind, sc in next 3 sts of R53 behind, hdc in next st of R53 behind, dc in next st of R53 behind**, skip 207 sts, (2dc, ch2, 2dc) in next st*, rep from * to * 2x and * to ** 1x, 2dc in same st as first sts, ch1, join with sc to 3rd ch of stch.
{161 sts on each side; 4 2-ch cnr sps}

R56: sc over joining sc, *sc in next 5 sts, 24x [sc in lbv of 4th st of the 7-st group of R54 & next st at the same time, sc in next 2 sts, fpsc around next st, sc in next 2 sts], sc in lbv of 4th st of the 7-st group of R54 & next st at the same time, sc in next 5 sts**, (sc, ch2, sc) in 2-ch cnr sp*, rep from * to * 2x and * to ** 1x, sc in same sp as first st, ch1, join with sc to first st.
{163 sts on each side; 4 2-ch cnr sps}

R57: ch3 (stch), dc over joining sc, *skip 1 st, 54x [skip 2 sts, dc in next st, dc in 2nd skipped st, dc in first skipped st]**, (2dc, ch2, 2dc) in 2-ch cnr sp*, rep from * to * 2x and * to ** 1x, 2dc in same sp as first sts, ch1, join with sc to 3rd ch of stch. {166 sts on each side; 4 2-ch cnr sps}

R58: sc over joining sc, *sc in next 2 sts, 54x [sc between last and next sts, sc in next 3 sts], sc between last and next sts, sc in next 2 sts**, (sc, ch2, sc) in 2-ch cnr sp*, rep from * to * 2x and * to ** 1x, sc in same sp as first st, ch1, join with sc to first st.
{223 sts on each side; 4 2-ch cnr sps}

R59: ch3 (stch), dc over joining sc, *dc in next st, fptr around next 2 sts of R57, skip 2 sts, 54x [hdc in next st, fptr3tog around and over next 3 sts of R57, skip 3 sts], hdc in next st, fptr around next 2 sts of R57, skip 2 sts, dc in next st**, 3dc in 2-ch cnr sp*, rep from * to * 2x and * to ** 1x, dc in same sp as first sts, join with ss to 3rd ch of stch. {115 sts on each side; 4 3-st cnrs}

R60: ch3 (stch), dc in same st as ss, *fpdc around next 4 sts, 54x [dc in next st, (dc in, fpdc around) next st], dc in next st, fpdc around next 4 sts**, 3dc in next st*, rep from * to * 2x and * to ** 1x, dc in same st as first sts, join with ss to 3rd ch of stch.
{171 sts on each side; 4 3-st cnrs}

R61: ch3 (stch), dc in same st as ss, *fpdc around next 5 sts, skip 1 st, sc in next st, 26x [skip 2 sts, 7dc in next st, skip 2 sts, sc in next st], skip 2 sts, 7dc in next st, skip 1 st, sc in next st, fpdc around next 5 sts**, 3dc in next st*, rep from * to * 2x and * to ** 1x, dc in same st as first sts, join with ss to 3rd ch of stch. {227 sts on each side; 4 3-st cnrs}

R62: ch3 (stch), dc in same st as ss, *fpdc around next 6 sts, 27x [fpsc around next st, fpdc around next 7 sts], fpsc around next st, fpdc around next 6 sts**, 3dc in next st*, rep from * to * 2x and * to ** 1x, dc in same st as first sts, join with ss to 3rd ch of stch.
{229 sts on each side; 4 3-st cnrs}

R63: *Note: the stitches along the side are all worked into R61 sts behind R62.* ch3 (stch), dc in same st as ss, *fpdc around next 7 sts, dc2tog over next 2 sts of R61 behind, 26x [hdc in next st of R61 behind, sc in next 3 sts of R61 behind, hdc in next st of R61 behind, dc3tog over next 3 sts of R61 behind], hdc in next st of R61 behind, sc in next 3 sts of R61 behind, hdc in next st of R61 behind, dc2tog over next 2 sts of R61 behind, fpdc around next 7 sts**, 3dc in next st*, rep from * to * 2x and * to ** 1x, dc in same st as first sts, join with ss to 3rd ch of stch. {177 sts on each side; 4 3-st cnrs}

R64: sc in same st as ss, *sc in next 11 sts, 26x [sc in lbv of 4th st of the 7-st group of R62 & next st at the same time, sc in next 2 sts, 2sc in next st, sc in next 2 sts], sc in lbv of 4th st of the 7-st group of R62 & next st at the same time, sc in next 11 sts**, (sc, ch2, sc), in next st*, rep from * to * 2x and * to ** 1x, sc in same st as first st, ch1, join with sc to first st.
{207 sts on each side; 4 2-ch cnr sps}

R65: ch3 (stch), *dc in next 207 sts**, (dc, ch2, dc) in 2-ch cnr sp*, rep from * to * 2x and * to ** 1x, dc in same sp as first st, ch1, join with sc to 3rd ch of stch.
{209 sts on each side; 4 2-ch cnr sps}

R66: sc over joining sc, *sc in next 209 sts**, (sc, ch2, sc), in next st*, rep from * to * 2x and * to ** 1x, sc in same st as first st, ch1, join with sc to first st. {211 sts on each side; 4 2-ch cnr sps}

R67: ch3 (stch), *dc in next 211 sts**, (dc, ch2, dc) in 2-ch cnr sp*, rep from * to * 2x and * to ** 1x, dc in same sp as first st, ch1, join with sc to 3rd ch of stch.
{213 sts on each side; 4 2-ch cnr sps}

R68: ch3 (stch), *106x [fpdc around next st, hdc in next st], fpdc around next st**, (dc, ch2, dc) in 2-ch cnr sp*, rep from * to * 2x and * to ** 1x, dc in same sp as first st, ch1, join with sc to 3rd ch of stch. {215 sts on each side; 4 2-ch cnr sps}

R69: ch4 (stch), (2trcl, ch2, 3trcl) over joining sc, *skip 1 st, fpdc around next st, 35x [dc in next 2 sts, starting in same st as last st fptr3tog over next 5 sts skipping the 2nd and 4th sts, dc in same st as last st], dc in next st, fpdc around next st, skip 1 st**, (2x [3trcl, ch2], 3trcl) in 2-ch cnr sp*, rep from * to * 2x and * to ** 1x, 3trcl in same sp as first sts, ch2, join with ss to top of 2trcl. {143 sts on each side; 4 (3-st & 2 2-ch sp) cnrs}

R70: sc in same st as ss, *2sc in 2-ch sp, 2sc in next st, fpdc around next st, dc in next 2 sts, 34x [ch2, skip 1 st, dc in next 3 sts], ch2, skip 1 st, dc in next 2 sts, fpdc around next st, 2sc in next st, 2sc in 2-ch sp**, (sc, ch2, sc) next st*, rep from * to * 2x and * to ** 1x, sc in same st as first st, ch1, join with sc to first st. {118 sts, 35 2-ch sps on each side; 4 2-ch cnr sps}

R71: sc over joining sc, *sc in next 5 sts, fpdc around next st, 35x [sc in next st, (2x [tr, ch2]) in cl of R69 below, fptr around same st, skip (1 st, 2-ch sp & 1 st)], sc in next st, fpdc around next st, sc in next 5 sts**, (sc, ch2, sc) in 2-ch cnr sp*, rep from * to * 2x and * to ** 1x, sc in same sp as first st, ch1, join with sc to first st. {155 sts on each side; 4 2-ch cnr sps}

R72: ch3 (stch), *dc in next 6 sts, fpdc around next st, 35x [dc in next st, htr in skipped st of R70 behind, 2htr in 2-ch sp of R70 behind, htr in next skipped st of R70 behind, skip (2x [1 st, ch2] & 1 st)], dc in next st, fpdc around next st, dc in next 6 sts**, (dc, ch2, dc) in 2-ch cnr sp*, rep from * to * 2x and * to ** 1x, dc in same sp as first st, ch1, join with sc to 3rd ch of stch. {192 sts on each side; 4 2-ch cnr sps}

R73: sc over joining sc, *sc in next 7 sts, fpdc around next st, sc in next 3 sts, 34x [sc in lbv of middle tr of R71 in front, sc in next 5 sts], sc in lbv of middle tr of R71 in front, sc in next 3 sts, fpdc around next st, sc in next 7 sts**, (sc, ch2, sc) in 2-ch cnr sp*, rep from * to * 2x and * to ** 1x, sc in same sp as first st, ch1, join with sc to first st.
{229 sts on each side; 4 2-ch cnr sps}

R74: sc over joining sc, *sc2tog over next 2 sts, sc in next 10 sts, 34x [sc2tog over next 2 sts, sc in next 4 sts], sc2tog over next 2 sts, sc in next 11 sts**, (sc, ch2, sc) in 2-ch cnr sp*, rep from * to * 2x and * to ** 1x, sc in same sp as first st, ch1, join with sc to first st.
{195 sts on each side; 4 2-ch cnr sps}

R75: ch3 (stch), *dc in next 195 sts**, (dc, ch2, dc) in 2-ch cnr sp*, rep from * to * 2x and * to ** 1x, dc in same sp as first st, ch1, join with sc to 3rd ch of stch.
{197 sts on each side; 4 2-ch cnr sps}

R76: sc over joining sc, *sc in next 197 sts**, (sc, ch2, sc) in 2-ch cnr sp*, rep from * to * 2x and * to ** 1x, sc in same sp as first st, ch1, join with sc to first st. {199 sts on each side; 4 2-ch cnr sps}

R77: ch3 (stch), dc over joining sc, *66x [ch1, skip 1 st, dc in next 2 sts], ch1, skip 1 st**, (2dc, ch2, 2dc) in 2-ch cnr sp*, rep from * to * 2x and * to ** 1x, 2dc in same sp as first sts, ch1, join with sc to 3rd ch of stch. {136 sts, 67 1-ch sps on each side; 4 2-ch cnr sps}

R78: ch3 (stch), *67x [fpdc around next 2 sts, ch1, skip 1-ch sp], fpdc around next 2 sts**, (dc, ch2, dc) in 2-ch cnr sp*, rep from * to * 2x and * to ** 1x, dc in same sp as first st, ch1, join with sc to 3rd ch of stch. {138 sts, 67 1-ch sps on each side; 4 2-ch cnr sps}

R79: ch3 (stch), *fpdc around next 3 sts, 66x [ch1, skip 1-ch sp, fpdc around next 2 sts], ch1, skip 1-ch sp, fpdc around next 3 sts**, (dc, ch2, dc) in 2-ch cnr sp*, rep from * to * 2x and * to ** 1x, dc in same sp as first st, ch1, join with sc to 3rd ch of stch.
{140 sts, 67 1-ch sps on each side; 4 2-ch cnr sps}

R80: ch3 (stch), *fpdc around next 4 sts, 66x [ch1, skip 1-ch sp, fpdc around next 2 sts], ch1, skip 1-ch sp, fpdc around next 4 sts**, (dc, ch2, dc) in 2-ch cnr sp*, rep from * to * 2x and * to ** 1x, dc in same sp as first st, ch1, join with sc to 3rd ch of stch.
{142 sts, 67 1-ch sps on each side; 4 2-ch cnr sps}

R81: ch3 (stch), *dc in next st, 2x [ch1, dc2tog over next 2 sts], skip 1-ch sp, 66x [ch2, dc3tog over next 2 sts and 1-ch sp], ch2, 2x [dc2tog over next 2 sts, ch1], dc in next st**, (dc, ch2, dc) in 2-ch cnr sp*, rep from * to * 2x and * to ** 1x, dc in same sp as first st, ch1, join with sc to 3rd ch of stch. {74 sts, 67 2-ch sps, 4 1-ch sps on each side; 4 2-ch cnr sps}

R82: sc over joining sc, *sc in next 2 sts, 2x [sc in 1-ch sp, sc in next st], 66x [2sc in 2-ch sp, sc in next st], 2sc in 2-ch sp, 2x [sc in next st, sc in 1-ch sp], sc in next 2 sts**, (sc, ch2, sc) in 2-ch cnr sp*, rep from * to * 2x and * to ** 1x, sc in same sp as first st, ch2, join with ss to first st. Fasten off. {214 sts on each side; 4 2-ch cnr sps}

Avalon
Charts

See page 120 for left-hand versions of the charts.

Avalon Rounds 1 - 22

Avalon Rounds 22 - 33

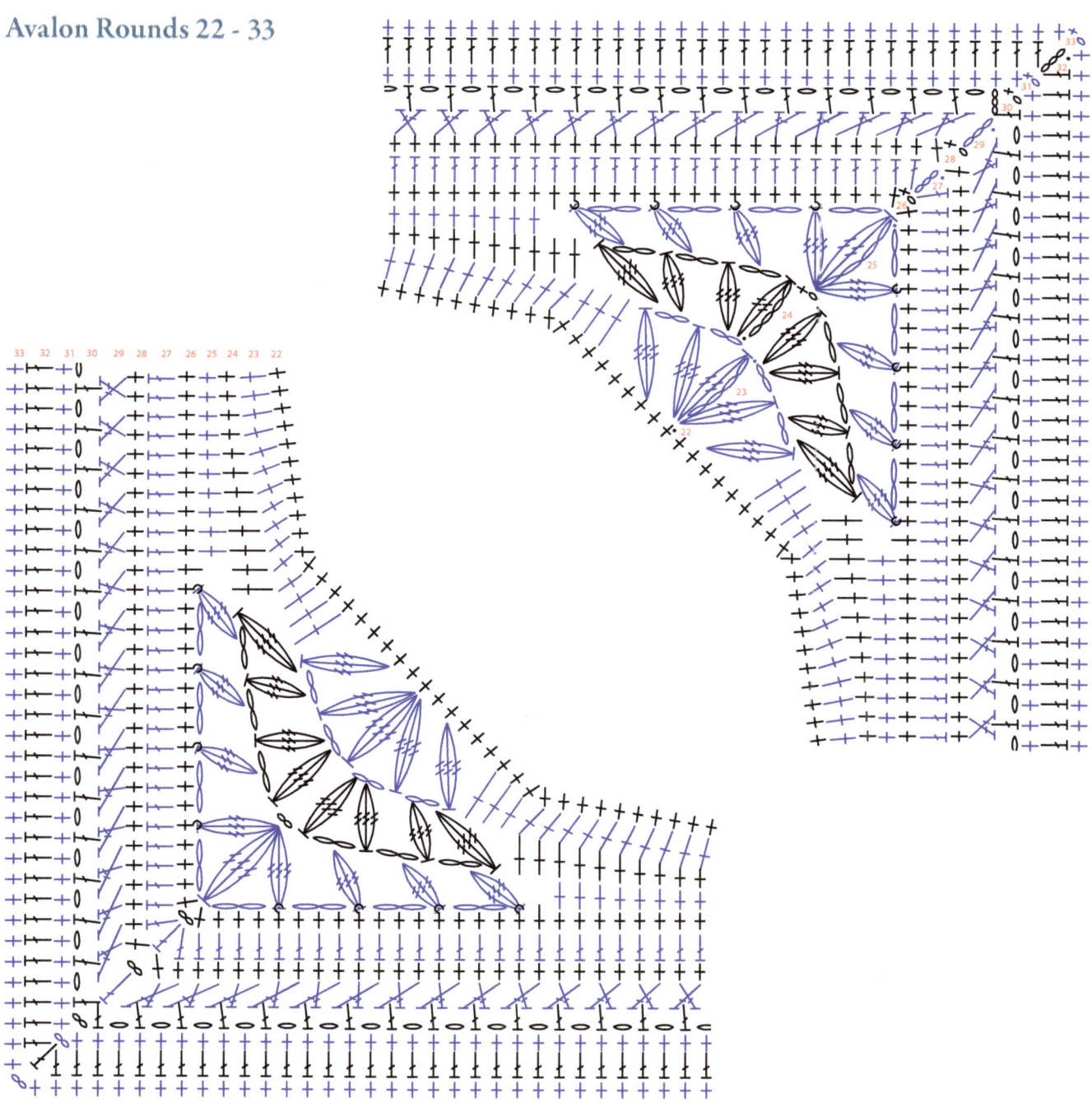

Avalon Rounds 33 - 49

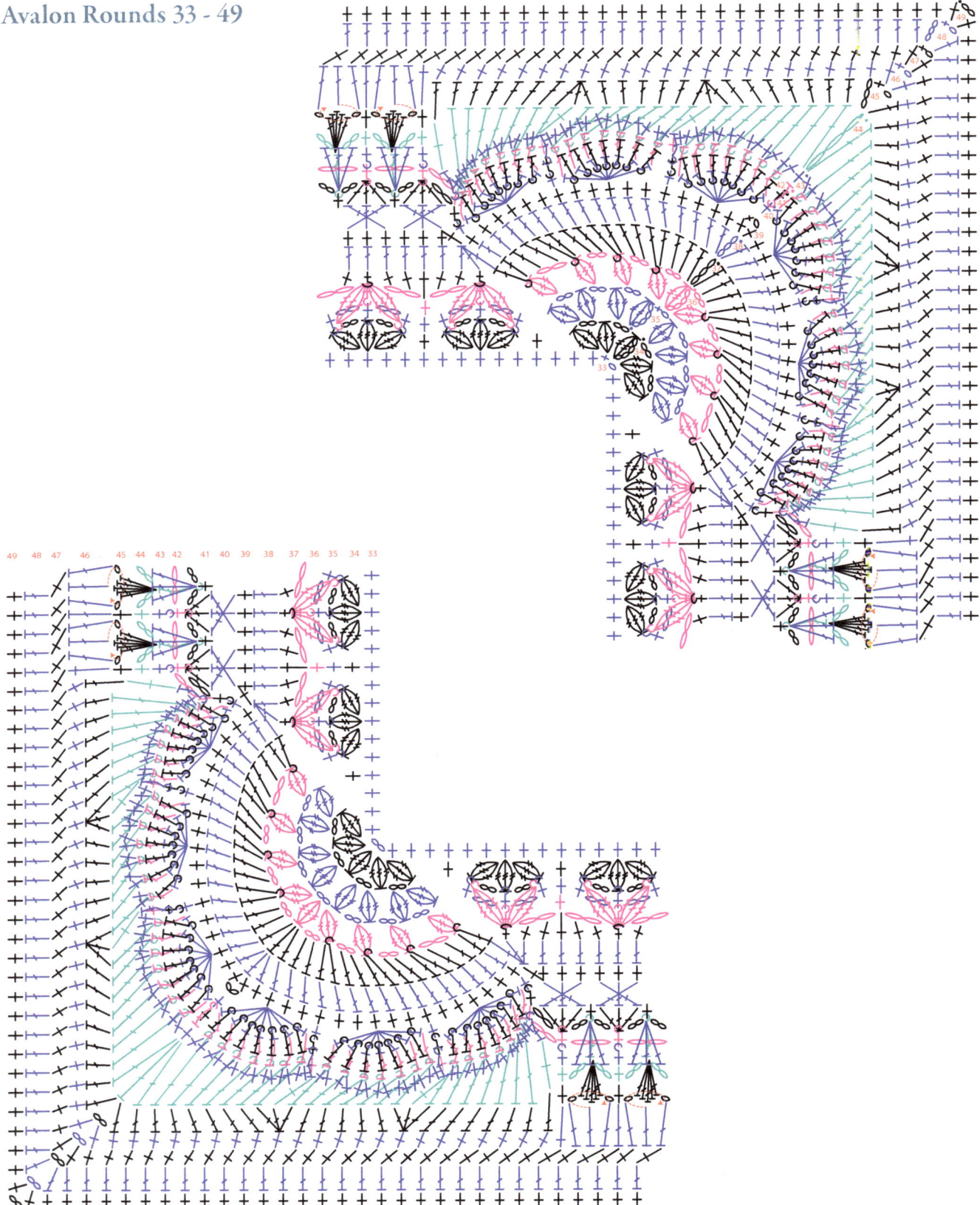

Caltha
Chart

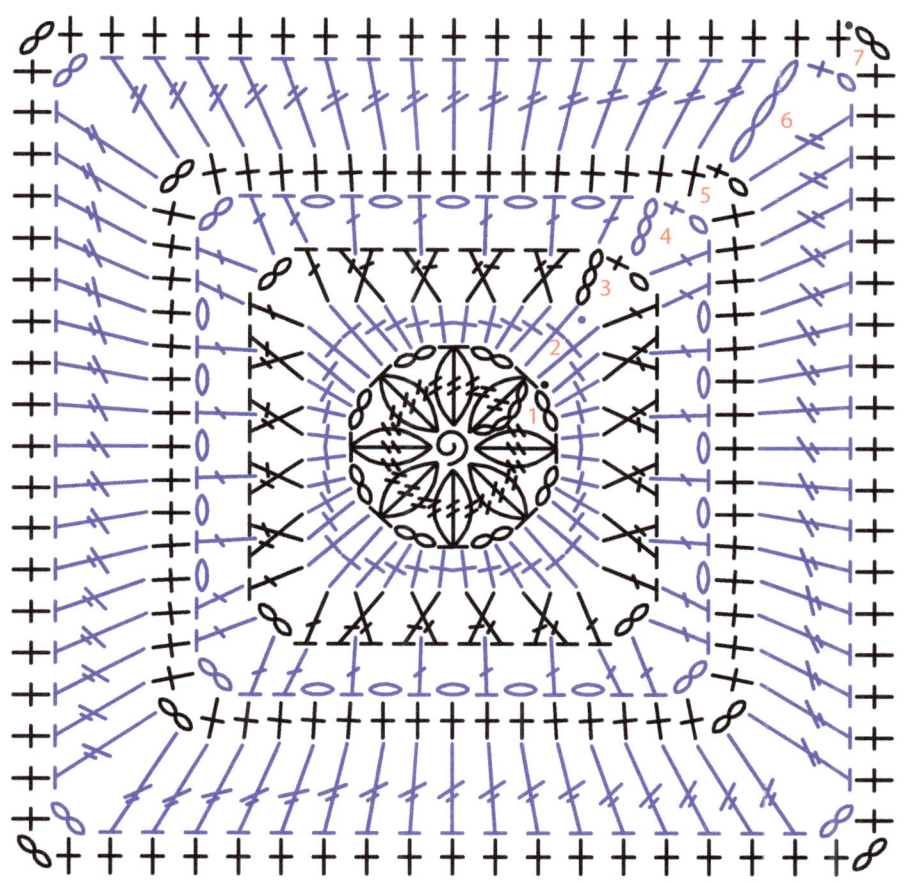

Caltha Rounds 1 - 7

Nimue
Charts

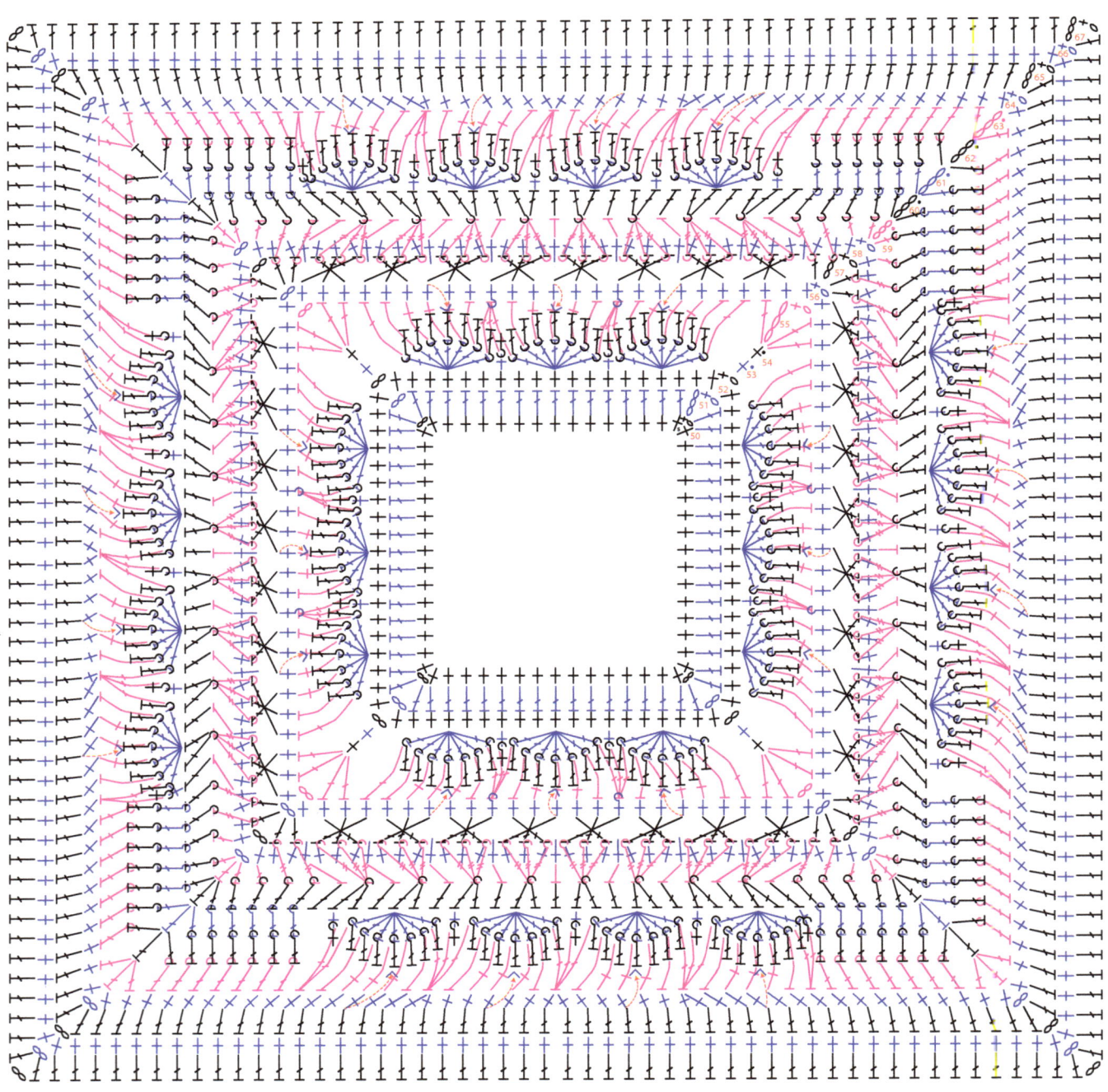

Nimue Rounds 50 - 67

Nimue Rounds 67 - 82

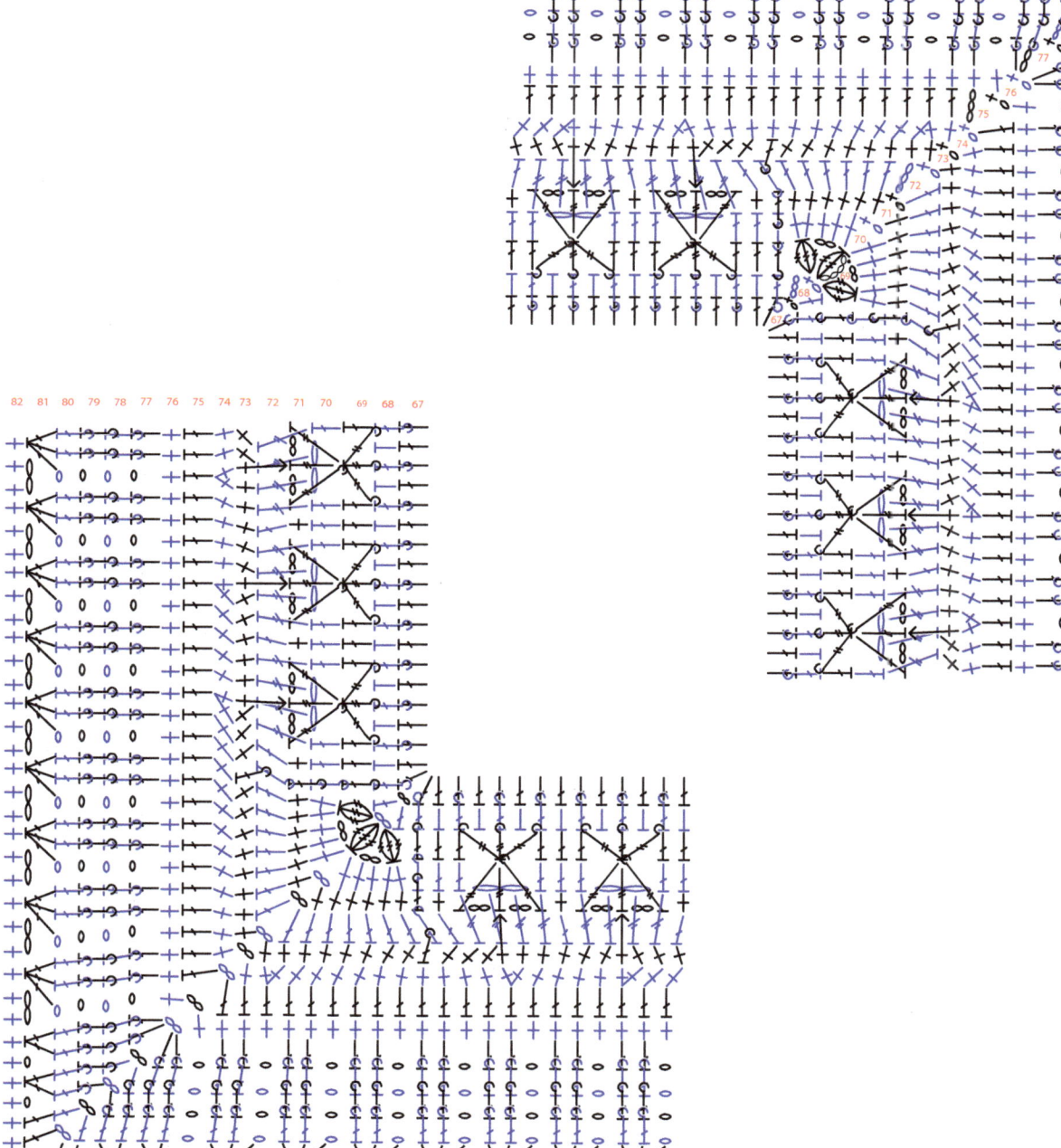

NIMUE'S COUNSEL

Here you will find extra help if you lose you way. Each round is covered with detailed photos and pearls of Nimue's wisdom to make sure you complete your quest unscathed.

Avalon
Round by Round Help

Round 1

As there are a lot of stitches in the first round, make sure you have a long tail for your magic circle.

The chain 1 at the start is not counted in the stitch count. It is there to help make it easier to find the first stitch of the round when you join up the round. It can still be hard to see, so pop a stitch marker in the first stitch of the round as soon as you make it.

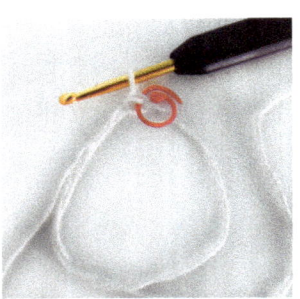

Round 2

Nothing hard here. After your initial chain 3 (or false stitch), chain 2 and work a stitch into the middle stitch of the 5-stitch group. Then chain 2 again and a stitch in the stitch between the 5-stitch groups.

Round 3

This is an easy round. One stitch in each stitch and 3 stitches in each 2-chain space. Again, if the first stitch of the round is hard to find, pop a stitch marker in it as soon as you've made it.

Round 4

Another easy one. All the same stitches. There are 2 in the first stitch (and every stitch that was worked into a stitch), then 3 in each of the stitches that was worked into the chain spaces. Check your stitch count is 40!

Round 5

You don't need me for this one – a stitch in each stitch. Easy.

Don't stress about it being a bit bowled or cupped. The next few rounds sort it out.

Round 6

OK. Now we get to an interesting round. What you'll be doing is working a stitch in every second stitch of Round 5 and a stitch around every second Round 4 stitch, working one chain between every stitch.

Here's where to work your first front post stitch.

Then you skip the stitch behind it, and work a stitch into the next stitch of Round 5.

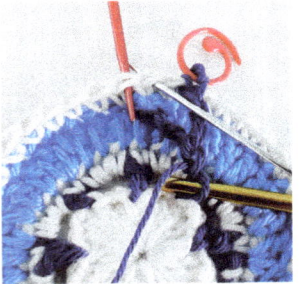

The silver needle is in the skipped stitch. The red needle is in the stitch to be worked into.

Round 7

You can do this one. Just remember that you are working front post stitches around the front post stitches and stitches into the regular stitches as well as a stitch in every 1-chain space.

The thing to watch out for is not to miss the stitch in the 1-chain space after you work the front post stitch.

The silver needle in is the 1-chain space you need to work a stitch into.

So there should be 3 stitches between each front post stitch.

Round 8

This round may have you learning a new trick! We are going to use the same stitch of Round 7 3 times in our repeat.

When you get to the front post stitches of Round 7, you'll be working a front post stitch around it, a stitch into it, and then another stitch around it. It gives you a Y shape that's pretty cool.

The red needle shows where to work the front post stitch and the silver needle shows where to work the stitch into the same stitch.

Here's what it looks like after the first front post stitch is made. You may need to pull the front post stitch down the stitch to see where to work the stitch into the same stitch.

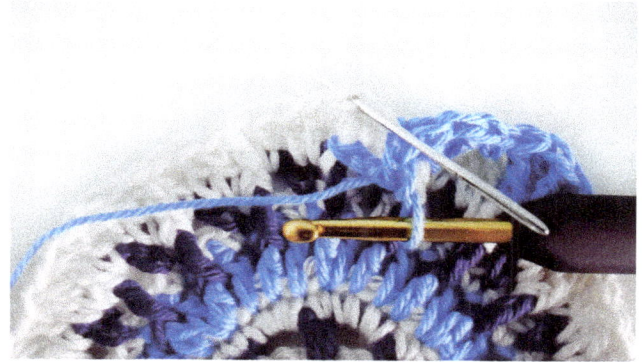

After you've worked your stitch in the stitch, you work another front post stitch around the same stitch. The red needle shows you where.

Then you skip a stitch (silver needle) and work a single stitch into the next stitch (red needle).

Round 9

Now this round will be VERY ruffled. Don't be alarmed. Magic will happen in the next round.

Once again, you'll be using the same stitch twice a couple of times, but the rest is easy. Think of the front post stitches of Round 8 as a large V shape. When you get to the right front post of the "V" (left for left-handed folks), you will work a front post stitch around it, as well as a stitch into it. Red needle shows around, silver in.

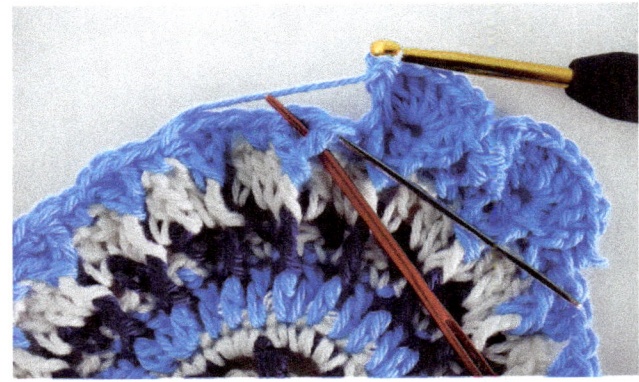

Then, you chain 1 and work 5 stitches into the stitch in the middle of the V and another chain 1.

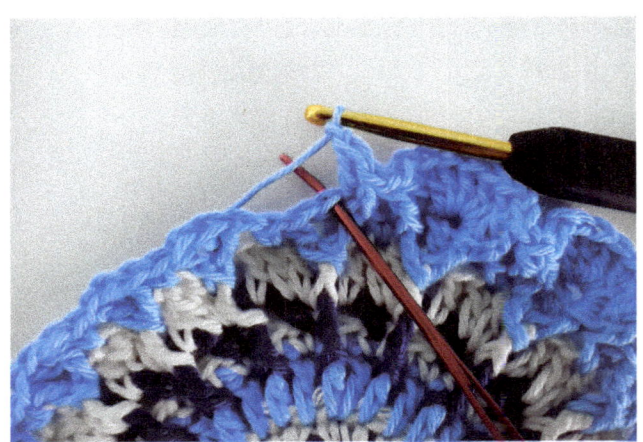

After that, you work a stitch in and then around the next stitch. Red needle in, silver around.

At the end of the repeat, you work a stitch into the stitch between the last and next front post stitches.

That's it! As I say, ruffled!

Round 10

Here's where the magic happens, where your circle will becomes nice and flat again.

There are a couple of quirks to this round. You'll be gathering those 5 stitches into one (like a popcorn) and also merging the front post stitches with a single front post stitch.

The first instruction is a little different. The chain 1 at the start does not count as a stitch in the stitch count. It's there to make it easier to work the first front post stitch. That front post stitch is worked around the last front post stitch of Round 9 and the first at the same time. You poke your hook under the front post stitches as shown by the red needle here:

Then, you work a stitch into the next stitch and then, poke your hook under the 5-stitch group, going in the 1-chain spaces either side of the 5 stitches, as shown by the red needle.

After that, it's a stitch in the next stitch, before we gather the front post stitches together again for the start of our repeat.

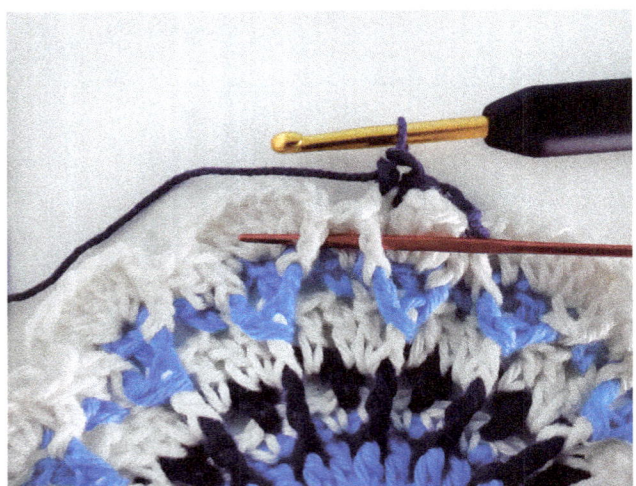

And at the end, it should look like this:

Round 11

You don't need me! Just a stitch in every stitch. Pop a stitch marker in the first stitch as soon as you make it, then count your stitches as you make them to make sure you have 80.

Round 12

Another easy one, a stitch, chain 2, skip one stitch, then another stitch. Easy.

Don't worry if it's a little cupped.

Round 13

Another interesting one! We're going to be working 2 front post stitches around each stitch, with 2 chains between them, and working 2 stitches in every 2-chain space.

At the start, we need to get our hook to the right spot, so you need to do a front post slip stitch. Don't be daunted. Just poke your hook where the red needle is and work a slip stitch.

Then, work your chain 3 (or false stitch), chain 2 and then another front post stitch around the same stitch.

Then it's 2 stitches in the 2-chain space, before you do your next front post stitch.

Here's what it looks like at the end of the first full repeat. Make sure you work 2 chains between your front post stitches that are worked around the same stitch.

At the end of the round, make sure you join to either the top of the 3rd chain of your starting chain or your false stitch if you made one.

Round 14

In this round, we'll be sometimes working a stitch in and around a stitch like we've done before.

After your starting chain (or false stitch), in the 2 chain space, you work 5 stitches, then it's time to work a stitch into and another around the next stitch.

The red needle shows where to work into the stitch and the silver, where to work around it.

The next bit is easy – you skip the next 3 stitches and work a single stitch into the next 2-chain space.

The red needle shows where to work the single stitch in the 2-chain space and the silver, the next lot of 5 stitches.

Then, you work a stitch around and in the next stitch before we go back to 5 stitches in the 2-chain space.

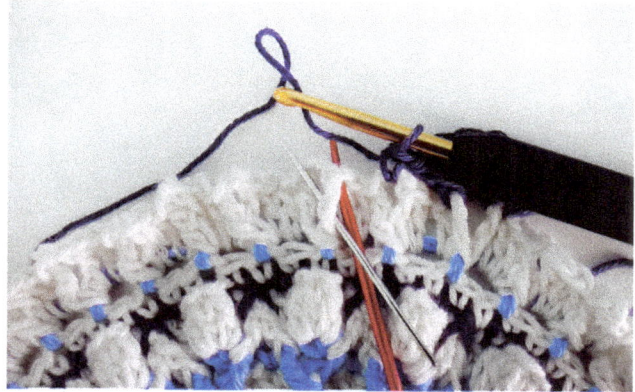

Silver shows around and red shows in. Work the front post stitch first, then the stitch in the same stitch.

So in the 2-chain spaces, you're alternating between 5 stitches and 1 stitch in them.

Don't forget the last front post stitch around the same stitch you worked your starting chain or false stitch around, before you join with a slip stitch to your 3rd chain of starting chain or false stitch.

Round 15

Now instead of working a stitch in the same stitch as your slip stitch of the last round, you're going to begin the repeat straight away by working a stitch in the next 2 stitches – the first 2 stitches of the 5-stitch group worked into the 2-chain space.

Silver needle shows the stitch to skip and the red one, where to work your first of 2 stitches.

Then it's 3 stitches in the middle one and 2 stitches into the last 2 of the 5-stitch group.

Silver shows where to work the 3 stitches and the red where to work the first of the 2 stitches.

Now the fun bit. After skipping one stitch, you're going to be joining the next 2 front post stitches together, ignoring the stitch between them. How do you do that? Easy! Poke your hook under both front post stitches and work a front post stitch (as shown by the red needle). Job done.

Then skip a stitch and you're back to the start of the repeat.

 *Nimue's Decree*

You do not join this round at all.

Round 16

The first stitch of this round is a bit fiddly to do, but it's just one stitch. You can do it. You work it into the last stitch of Round 15 – the one you just made before not joining the round. The red needle is pointing to where to poke your hook.

After that, it's easy! Chain 5 then skip the "petal" and work a stitch in the stitch between the "petals", as shown by the red needle.

Don't worry about the chains being in front if that happens for you. Simply pull the petals through to the front once you're done.

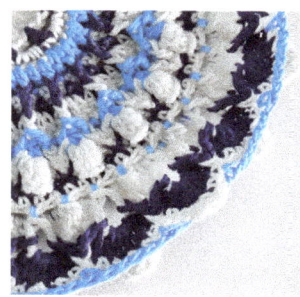 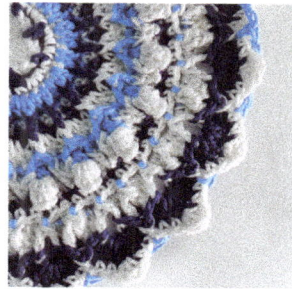

Round 17

Another easy one! We start with 4 stitches (including the starting chain or false stitch) in the same stitch as the slip stitch, then we begin the repeat. A single stitch in the 5-chain space, then 7 stitches in the next stitch.

Red needle shows where to work the single stitch into the chain space and the silver, where to work the 7 stitches.

Finish with 3 more stitches in the same stitch as the first stitches were worked into before joining with a slip stitch.

Round 18

In this round, we go from 20 pointy bits to 10. Here's how.

Begin with your starting chain or false stitch, then work another stitch in the same stitch as your slip stitch join of Round 17. Then you work 2 stitches in each of the next 3 stitches.

The silver needle shows where to work the single stitch into the middle stitch of a 7-stitch group and the red one, where to work the first of the 2 stitches in the next 3 stitches.

Now, skip 4 stitches and work a single stitch into what should be the middle stitch of a 7-stitch group.

Then skip 4 again and work 2 stitches in each of the next 3 stitches, and then in the next stitch (the middle one of a 7-stitch group), work 2 stitches, chain 2 and 2 more stitches (red needle in photo). And you're back to the start of the repeat.

At the end, instead of joining with a slip stitch, I tell you to chain 1 then join with a stitch to the 3rd chain of the starting chain or false stitch. What this does is place your hook as if it was in the middle of a 2-chain point – exactly where you need to be to start the next round.

Start with chain 2 as your starting chain. False stitch folks; don't try to work a half stitch false stitch here – it's way too fiddly and in this round, chain 2 works best.

Then we start the repeat with a half stitch in next 8 stitches and when you come to the stitch in the dip between points, you work a slip stitch in that dip stitch.

 Nimue's Decree

The slip stitch in the repeat does count as a stitch in the stitch count.

Then, work another half stitch in the next 8 stitches and one in the 2-chain space.

At the end of the round, we're going to join with an invisible join. You can do it!

First, cut your yarn and pull the loop on your hook up so the end comes free.

Round 19

This round is easy but may end in a way that's new to you.

Thread that end onto a yarn needle and poke it under the v of the first real stitch of the round – the first half stitch after the chain 2.

Then poke it back through the top of the last half stitch you made and also through the loop behind the v on the back.

Front   *Back*

Pull it slowly until a v the same size as your regular stitches appears on top of the chain 2, creating a seamless edge. You have just made an invisible join. Go you.

 Nimue's Counsel

Don't weave the end in properly yet as it will make the next round harder than it has to be.

Round 20

In this round, you'll be working all your stitches into the "lbv" or loop behind v. It's also known as the 3rd loop or back bump.

Have a close look at your stitches before you start. The red needle is showing a lbv where you'll be poking your hook.

At the start of the round, we need to re-attach our yarn. You do that by working a standing stitch. A standing stitch is how you can attach yarn using any stitch as a proper stitch from the very start. In this case, we're making a 2 stitches together type of cluster.

Here's how:

Attach your yarn to your hook with a slip knot, while holding the loop on the hook firmly, yarn over and poke your hook into the loop behind v of the stitch before a slip stitch in the dip between points and pull through a loop.

Then we begin the repeat, working all your stitches into the loop behind v of every stitch.

 Nimue's Counsel

The 4th stitch of the set of 7 stitches should fall in the loop behind v of the stitch worked into the 2-chain space of Round 18.

Yarn over and pull through 2 loops on your hook. Skip the slip stitch in the dip. Yarn over and poke your hook into the loop behind v of the next stitch and pull up a loop. Yarn over and pull through 2 loops on your hook, then yarn over and complete the stitch by pulling through all 3 loops on the hook.

✱ *Nimue's Counsel*

When you join with a slip stitch to the standing stitch, after you have inserted your hook into the standing stitch, make sure you place your yarn in front of the slip knot as you work your slip stitch. Doing this, forces the knot of the slip knot to the back.

Round 21

Another easy round. The only thing to watch for is to make sure you do 2 stitches in the 2-together stitch.

Probably a good idea to check your stitch count at this point too. You should have 170 stitches.

✱ *Nimue's Counsel*

If you're like me and lose count easily, pop a stitch marker in every 10th or 20th stitch so you don't have to start from the beginning again when you do lose count.

Round 22

This is an easy round, but you do need to pay attention. This is how I keep track:

Do your first 8 stitches for the start, then once you hit the "*2 stitches in next stitch", start counting up to 18, remembering that the first and second stitches are worked into the same stitch and 3 to 18 are worked as one stitch in each stitch.

2 stitches in one, then 16 on their own makes 18

Round 23

Here is where we begin to square off the circle. From now on, we'll be starting and ending each round in the middle of a corner. That means we work half a corner at the start and complete the corner at the end of the round. Doing it this way helps it all look seamless.

The corner in this case is made up of clusters made of large stitches. You can begin as written and do chain 4 plus a 2-stitch cluster to take the place of your first cluster, or if you're used to doing false stitches, make a full 3-stitch cluster from the start. I did it with chain 4 and a 2-stitch cluster in the video for Round 23 and as a false stitch cluster in the video for Round 24.

❋ *Nimue's Counsel*

> **Confused by all the different brackets? Don't be. Break it down. Everything between the [ ] brackets is worked into one stitch. So work the 2x ( ) instructions, then the last cluster all in the same stitch.**

Once you wrap your head around the corners, the sides are really easy. Just make sure you skip a stitch before and after your corner set of clusters and chains.

At the end of the round, if you did a chain 4 starting chain, don't join to the top of the 4th chain, rather, join to the top of the 2-stitch cluster. That makes the starting chain and first cluster mimic a 3-stitch cluster better.

Join to where the red needle is pointing, not the silver one.

Round 24

This round is very similar to the last one, except the clusters are all worked into the 2-chain spaces. That's why you need to slip stitch into the next 2-chain space at the start.

Each 2-chain space has 2 3-stitch clusters separated by a 2-chain space. There is no 2-chain space before the first cluster, nor after the last cluster.

✳ *Nimue's Counsel*

Don't worry about the larger than normal top of that first cluster. Once the pattern is complete, you won't notice it. If it does bother you, it is possible to reduce it a bit by keeping your finger firmly on the loop on the hook and the 2 yarn overs made at the start of the stitch as you make the complete 3-stitch cluster.

At the end of the round, you need to complete your first corner clusters. The difference being you don't work chain 2 before joining the round. Instead, you will chain 1 and join with a stitch to place your hook in the exact spot to begin the next round.

Round 25

One more round of clusters as corners. This time, you're working just one cluster in the 2-chain space, but in the middle 2-chain space of the corner, you will work 3 clusters with 2-chain spaces between them.

At the start, we'll again either do a starting chain and 2-stitch cluster, or a false stitch 3-stitch cluster over the joining stitch. Then you chain 2 and make another 3-stitch cluster over the joining stitch. And that's the start of your first corner done.

Now we move on to the next lot of clusters. Chain 2 and work a cluster in each of the 2-chain spaces, skipping the clusters of Round 24. Don't do 2 chains after the last one.

The sides are easy! Skip 3 stitches and work a stitch in 24 stitches, skip 3 more stitches and it's back to clusters in 2-chain spaces again. The corner is cluster, chain 2, cluster, chain 2, cluster in the middle 2-chain space of the corner.

✱ *Nimue's Counsel*

Make sure you have 9 clusters and 8 2-chain spaces around all of your corners.

At the end of the round, make one more cluster in the same 2-chain space as the first clusters, chain 2 and join with a slip stitch to the top of your 2-stitch cluster if you did a starting chain, or your 3-stitch cluster if you did a false stitch cluster.

Round 26

A few easy rounds now! Phew.

Start with a stitch in the same stitch as your slip stitch, then work 3 stitches in each 2-chain space, and a front post stitch around each of the clusters.

Red needle shows where to poke your hook to make the first front post stitch.

After your last front post stitch, before you start the stitches in stitches for the side, work a stitch between the cluster and the next stitch. Do that before your first cluster heading back to the corner.

The red needle shows where to work a stitch between the stitches and the silver needle shows where to work the stitch after that.

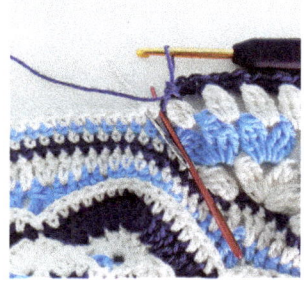 

Your corner is a stitch, chain 2 and stitch in the middle corner cluster.

* *Nimue's Counsel*

    If you have trouble reading your stitches, pop a scrap of yarn in the gap before you join with a stitch. That will show you where to work the first and last stitches of the next round.

Round 27

Start with your chain 3 or false stitch then work a stitch over the joining stitch. The scrap of yarn shows you where to place your hook to do that.

You don't need me for the rest of this round. A stitch in every stitch and 3 stitches in every 2-chain corner space.

End with another stitch in the same space as the first stitches (where the scrap of yarn is) and the slip stitch join.

Round 28

This one is oh so easy! A stitch in every stitch and the corners are a stitch, chain 2 and a stitch. Remember the scrap of yarn tip if you have trouble seeing the joining stitch for the next round.

Round 29

OK. Time for another fun round. The same stitches are used all the way around, it's just where they are worked is a bit different.

Begin with your starting chain or false stitch, then, skip one stitch, work a stitch in the next one, then work a stitch in the stitch you skipped.

Red needle shows the stitch to skip, the silver where to work your first stitch.

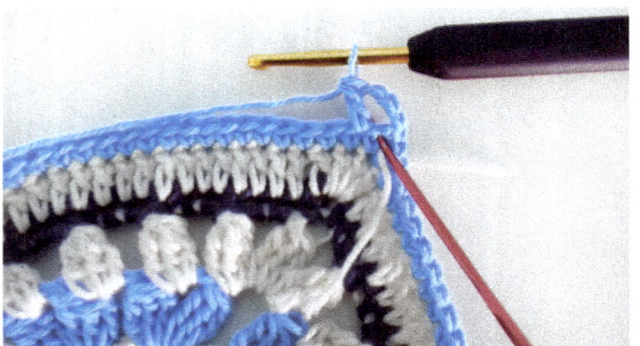

Now work a stitch where the red needle is, in the skipped stitch.

It creates an "X" shape. Do that all the way along. The thing to watch for is to make sure you are skipping a stitch as it can look like the next stitch is free, when really it was used to make the first part of the last "X".

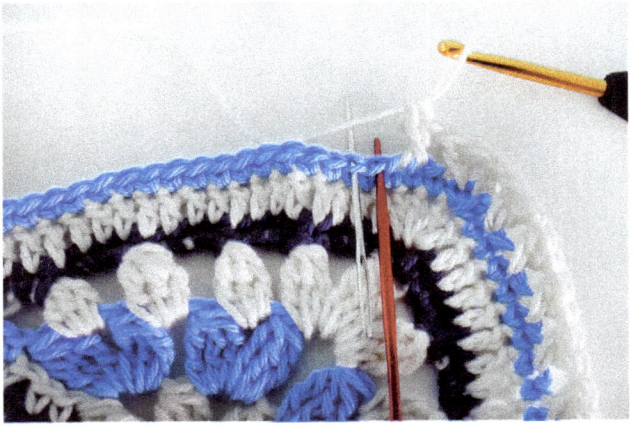

The corners of this round are just one stitch worked into the 2-chain corner spaces.

✸ *Nimue's Counsel*

Make sure you have 32 "X" shapes along each side.

Round 30

All the same stitches again this time and you'll be working most of the stitches between stitches rather than into them.

Start as you have been, then chain 1 and work a stitch between the 2 stitches of the first "X". Chain 1 and do the same all the way along.

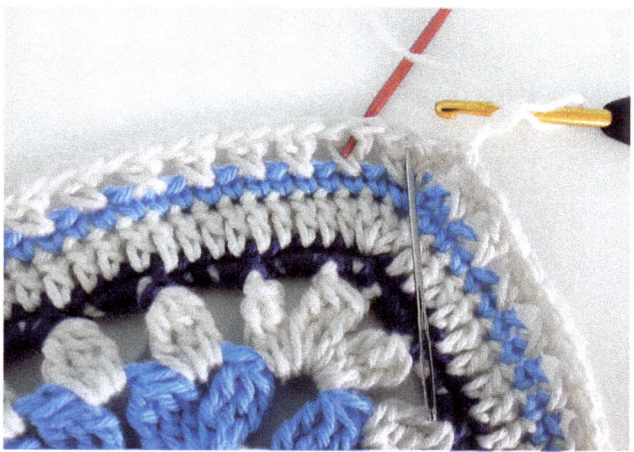

Both needles show where to work stitches between the "X" stitches.

After the last stitch in the middle of the "X", chain 1 then work your corner (1 stitch, chain 2, 1 stitch) in the corner stitch.

Round 31

This one is easy! A stitch in every stitch and chain space plus your usual corners in the 2-chain corner space. Nothing new here.

Round 32

This one is the same as Round 27, just with more stitches along the side. You've got this.

Round 33

Once again, nothing new – the same as Round 28 with more stitches along the sides again.

Round 34

Alrighty! Are you ready to make LOTS of clusters? The corners of this round are similar, but not exactly the same as the corners of Round 23. This time all the corner clusters are worked into the 2-chain corner spaces. There are 5 clusters in each corner space, separated by 2-chain spaces.

Be careful you note the very first stitch of the side as it can be covered by the clusters in the corner – the red needle is showing that first stitch to skip. The silver needle shows where to work your first side stitch.

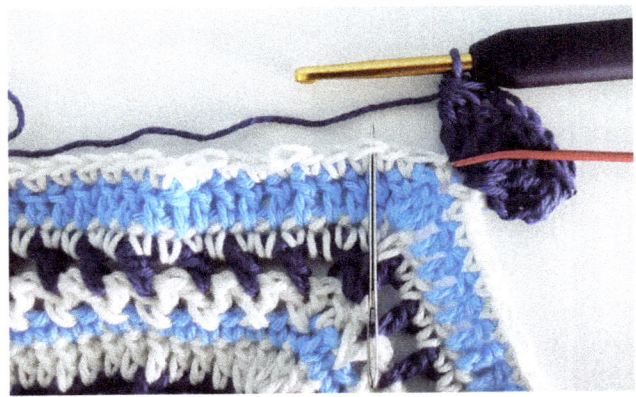

Once you've started your corner, it's time for the side repeat to start. This is where what I call the donuts start. After you skip 3 stitches and work your first stitch of the side, you skip 2 stitches then work 3 clusters separated by 2-chain spaces in the next stitch. Yes. Cluster, chain 2, cluster, chain 2, cluster – all in the same stitch. Then skip 2 stitches followed by a single stitch in your next stitch.

You will end up with 11 groups of 3 clusters along each side.

Yes, I know. It'll take some time. You can do it! Pop on a show to watch.

Round 35

OK, there are a lot of instructions for this round, but you can do it. Break it down. First, you'll start with your corner clusters – 2 clusters separated by a 2-chain space in each 2-chain space of Round 34. There will be 8 clusters and 7 2-chain spaces around each corner. Keep an eye on that as you work.

Now the side. Each set of 3 donut clusters followed by the next stitch is all you need to think about. First, skip 2 stitches after you've done your last corner cluster. The first stitch you skip will be the last cluster of Round 34 and the first side stitch is the second one you skip. Then you're up to your first side cluster.

The red needle shows where to work your first front post stitch after skipping 2 stitches.

The repeat is: front post stitch round the first cluster, chain 2, skip 2-chain space, back post stitch around the middle cluster, chain 2 and skip the 2-chain space, then a front post stitch around the last cluster. You finish with a stitch in the stitch between the cluster sets.

The red needle is showing where to work your back post stitch after chaining 2.

This time, the red needle is showing where to work the second front post stitch after chaining 2.

The last stitch of the side is the front post stitch around the last side cluster. Then you skip the last stitch of the side and the first corner cluster before you work your corner clusters.

Round 36

Another round of long instructions, as well as lots of clusters - again! This is almost the end of the donut creation. This round will look a little weird – don't worry, the next round makes it look all good again.

The corner clusters are as you have done before – one in each 2-chain space with 3 clusters separated by 2-chain spaces in the middle 2-chain corner space.

Now the side. Again, break it down to each donut on its own and you'll be fine.

At the start of the side instructions, you skip one stitch – that's the last corner cluster. Then you work a front post cluster around the cluster of Round 34.

The silver needle is in the last side cluster and the red one where you work your first front post cluster.

How to work a front post cluster:
Instead of poking your hook in a stitch to make the cluster, you work all 3 legs of the cluster around the cluster. It may feel strange, but it works.

Next, you go straight to working a back post stitch around the back post stitch of Round 35 – no chains, and then a front post cluster around the next cluster of Round 34.

The red needle shows where to work your back post stitch.

Then you work another front post cluster around the next cluster from Round 34.

Here is where you chain 2 and work a stitch in the stitch between the donuts, chain 2 and you're back to working the next donut section.

Pat yourself on the back. You did the trickiest bit of the pattern. Go you.

After your last donut, you are back to the corner clusters. The red needle in this photo shows the stitch to skip.

Round 37

This is the round where we complete the donuts. Nothing too hard!

As you work around the corner clusters, it's all pretty easy. The corners are 3 stitches in the middle corner cluster. You work 2 stitches in each 2-chain space and in each cluster, you work a stitch in it and a front post stitch around it.

This photo shows a stitch already worked into a cluster and the red needle shows where to work the front post stitch around it.

After your last front post stitch around the last of the corner clusters, it's time to move on to the donuts. What you're doing is gathering the 2 clusters of the donut together with one stitch. The red needle shows where to poke your hook.

Ignore the stitch between the 2 clusters.

Then it's an easy bit – 2 stitches in the 2-chain space, 1 stitch in the next stitch, then 2 stitches in the 2-chain space and back to the donuts.

At the end of the side you're again using the corner cluster stitches twice, but this time you're working a front post stitch first, then a stitch in that same cluster.

The red needle shows where to work the front post stitch.

The silver needle in these photos shows where to work the stitch into the stitch after you've worked the front post stitch.

✱ Nimue's Counsel

If you find it hard to see where to work your stitch into the stitch after working a front post stitch, pull the front post stitch just made down to open up the space in the stitch you need to work into.

Round 38

This round is pretty easy! There's a stitch in each stitch mostly. There are 2 places along the side where you will crochet 3 stitches together. The first leg of the first crochet 3-together stitch should fall in the last front post stitch around a Round 36 cluster. The red needle shows where the first leg goes and the silver, where the last leg goes.

The same goes for the crochet 3-together stitch after the 57 stitches along the side. The first and last stitches of the 3-together should fall with the last leg in the front post stitch around a Round 36 cluster.

The corners are 3 stitches worked into the middle corner stitch.

Round 39

Another easy one, this time with smaller stitches and crocheting 2-together stitches twice along the side.

The corners are a stitch, chain 2 and a stitch in the middle stitch of the corners.

With the first 2-together stitch, the first leg should be in the 3-together stitch. For the second one, the first leg should be in the last single stitch before the 3-together stitch.

Round 40

Now things get interesting again! Around the corners we'll be making 7-stitch shells and along the sides, making crossed stitches like we did in Round 29, but this time we'll be using 3 stitches to make the crosses.

The corners in this round are simply one stitch in the 2-chain corner spaces.

After and before the corners, you'll work 3 sets of skip 2, 7 stitches in the next stitch, skip 2 and a single stitch in the next stitch. Make sure you skip 2 and not 3 as the first can be hidden by the 7 stitches.

Here's how to make the 3-stitch crosses along the side. This photo shows 2 stitches have been skipped and a stitch has been worked in the next stitch. Then you work a stitch where the red needle is and then another where the silver needle is. Cross made.

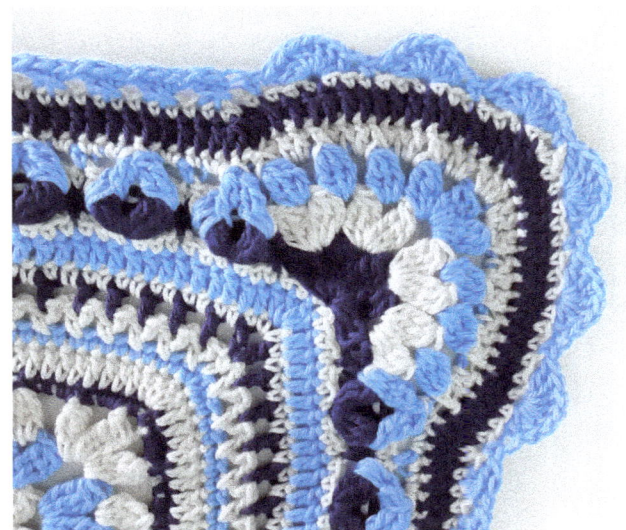

Round 41

Nothing too tricky in this round! Let's start with the curvy corners.

After your first stitch, three times you will work a front post stitch around each of the 7 shell stitches and the stitch between the shells. The stitch type is different. You work small stitches around the stitch in the dip between shells.

Then you chain 2 and work a stitch between the first and second cross like so:

The red needle shows the first stitch after the corner of 7 to work a front post stitch around and the silver needle where to work the small front post stitch.

Then you start the side. Remember the 3-stitch crosses in Round 40? Well, you are going to be working 3-together stitches over each of those crosses, along with some chains and stitches between the cross stitches.

You start with chain 2, then work your first 3-together stitches stitch over your first cross. The red needle shows where the first leg of your together stitch goes and the silver where the 3rd leg goes.

Chain 2 again and you're back to working your 3-together stitch.

At the end of the side, you chain 2, but you don't work a stitch between the last cross and the next stitch. Instead, the next stitch is the one you work your first small front post stitch around before the 7 front post stitches around the 3 shells.

The corners of Round 41 are a single stitch between the 3 sets of 7 shells.

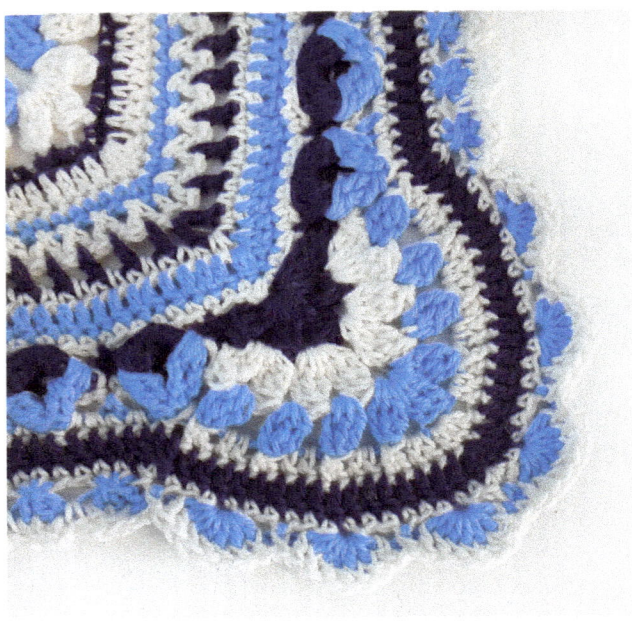

Round 42

There's a bit of working behind in this round and the corners are not a usual corner.

At the start, you need to make a front post stitch around the Round 40 corner stitch.

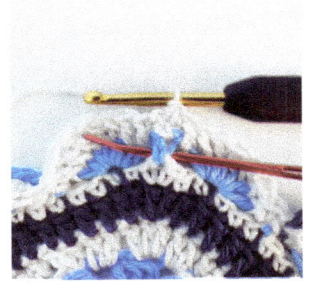 

In Round 41, we worked front post stitches around the sets of 7 shell stitches and the small stitches between them. Now you are going to work a stitch into each of the same Round 40 shell stitches, behind the front post stitches.

 *Nimue's Counsel*

Fold the front post stitches towards you to make it easy to see the Round 40 stitches behind.

When you get to the small stitches between the shells, work a stitch into the Round 41 stitch, not the Round 40 stitch behind.

Now the side bits are easy! The instructions are long, but simple. All you are doing is working a front post stitch around each of the 3-together stitches, chaining 2 between each one. Make sure you chain 2 before your first front post stitch and after your last one.

Round 43

A little bit of previous round work here, but not much.

After working your first stitch, three times you will work 2 stitches into the next 7 before you work a front post stitch around the small stitch between the shells of Round 40.

The first 2-chain space of the side is skipped, and you then work a front post stitch around the front post stitch of the last round. Next, you are working 3 stitches into the Round 41 stitch OVER the 2-chain space. That means you capture the chain in your 3 stitches. The chain space will not be visible.

Skip the last 2-chain space of the side before working your first front post stitch around the Round 41 stitch and 2 stitches in each of the next 7 shell stitches.

Round 44

Lots of going between rounds this time, but nothing too tricky. The corners of Round 44 are 3 stitches this time.

After starting your first corner, you work back post stitches around the 7 shell stitches in Round 42. This photo shows the first back post stitch made and the red needle is pointing to the stitch the second back post stitch will be worked around.

After the first lot of 7 back post stitches, you work a stitch into the Round 43 stitch between shells.

After your stitch in the Round 43 stitch after the third shell, it's time to start the side by working a stitch in the first front post stitch of the side. So in effect, you have a stitch worked into 2 consecutive stitches, then you chain 2 and work a back post stitch around the Round 41 stitch that has 3 stitches worked into it in Round 42.

The red needle is just showing in the photo, indicating where to work the back post stitch.

After the back post stitch, you chain 2 and work a stitch into the front post stitch after the next 3 stitches.

At the end of the side, you work a stitch in the last front post stitch of Round 43 then start the end of the side repeat. The red needle shows where to work the first stitch and the silver needle is just visible around the first stitch you will work a back post stitch around.

The corners are 3 stitches worked into the single stitch between the 2 sets of 3 shells.

Not much is visible on the front once you finish Round 44.

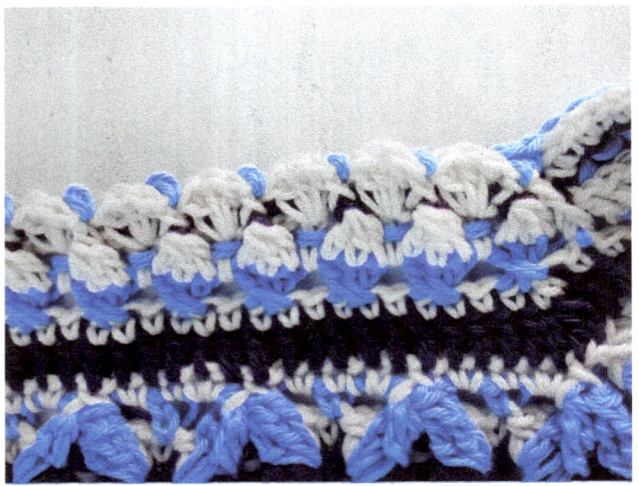

Round 45

This one is going to look quite funky along the sides. Trust that all will be well. The next round will make it all work.

We're beginning to square off Avalon now. The first and last parts of the side are pretty easy. Just a stitch in every stitch until you get to the dip between the shells. That's where you'll work 3-together stitch.

The needles show the first and last stitches of the 3 to be worked together.

Now, the sides!

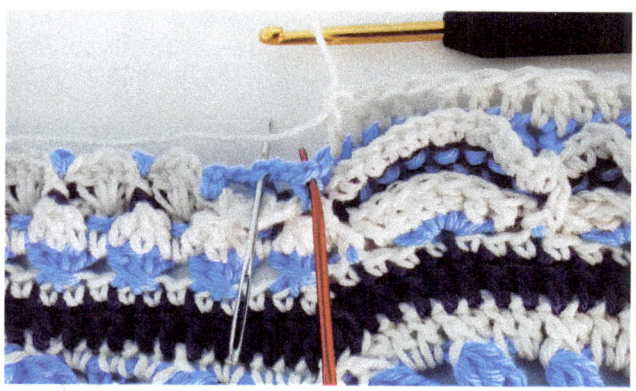

See how wobbly the sides are?

The red needle that's in the stitch before the first 2-chain space is where you work a stitch. Then, chain 1 and work 5 stitches into the stitch sitting behind the 3 stitches in one (silver needle). Chain 1, skip the 2-chain space and a stitch in the next one. And that's it! Just make sure you chain 1 between your sets of 5 and single stitches.

Don't forget that last stitch in stitch after your last set of 5 stitches and 1-chain space.

The corners this time are a stitch, chain 2 and a stitch in the middle stitch of the 3-stitch corner of Round 44. Easy.

Round 46

This is where the magic happens, and those wavy sides will be nice and flat again.

The corners and sides are easy. When you get to the first 1-chain space, work a stitch in it. Then you will work a single stitch in both 1-chain spaces either side of the 5-stitch group. So you poke your hook in the same 1-chain space you just worked a stitch into, under the 5 stitches and back out the 1-chain space on the other side to work your stitch. It feels like a post stitch, but you are really just using the 2 1-chain spaces at the same time. What this does is gather those 5 stitches into a popcorn shape.

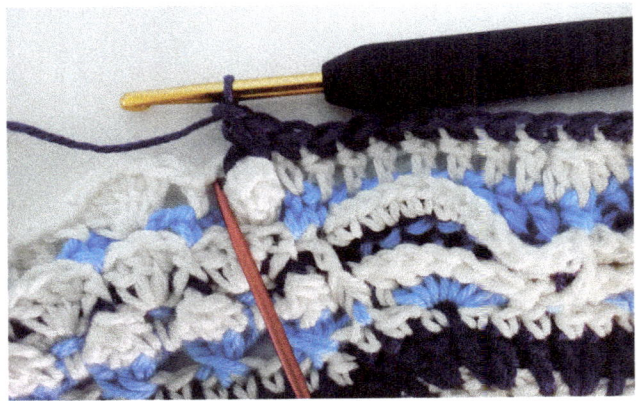

The red needle shows where to work the stitch in the same chain space after the stitch worked in both chain spaces.

Work a stitch in the single stitches between the 5-stitch sets.

The red needle is where you work the stitch into the 1-chain space and the silver needle shows where to poke your hook to work the stitch in both 1-chain spaces at the same time.

Round 47

Time to take a break from thinking and do some easy rounds.

This one is easy, you just need to skip some stitches along the side section above the popcorns. It's the stitches that you gathered the 5 stitches with you are skipping. The red needle shows the stitch to be skipped and the silver the next stitch to be worked into.

Round 48

You really don't need help for the next 2 rounds, as they are all simply a stitch in every stitch, with corners of one stitch, chain 2 and one stitch.

Round 49

Now it's time to leave the misty isle and waters of Avalon and head out into the verges of the lake with Caltha.

Caltha
Round by Round Help

Round 1

As there are a lot of stitches in the first round, make sure you have a long tail for your magic circle.

The instructions at the start – the chain 4 and 2-stitch cluster – take the place of a 3-stitch cluster. Once you have 8 2-chain spaces and 8 clusters, join with a slip stitch to the top of the 2-stitch cluster instead of the 4th chain of the starting chain. Doing this makes the starting chain plus the 2-stitch cluster mimic a 3-stitch cluster better.

The silver needle is pointing to the top of the 4th chain you'd usually join to and the red one to the top of the 2-stitch cluster where you need to join to.

Round 2

This round is really easy. Begin with a stitch in the same stitch you joined with a slip stitch, then work 3 stitches in every 2-chain space and 2 stitches in every cluster. End with a stitch in the same stitch as the first stitch was worked into.

 *Nimue's Counsel*

Do a false stitch at start to make a real cluster from the beginning as shown in the video.

✻ *Nimue's Counsel*

If you find it hard to identify the first stitch of the round, pop a stitch marker in the first stitch as soon as you make it.

Round 3

It may sound tricky at first glance, but once you see what's happening, it's easy enough. You just need to make sure you're skipping a stitch.

Begin with chain 3 starting chain or a false stitch. Now we begin the side of 4 crossed stitches. You skip a stitch, work a stitch in the next one, then go back and work a stitch in the stitch you skipped.

The silver needle is pointing to the stitch you skip and the red needle where to work your first stitch.

The silver needle shows where to work your stitch into the skipped stitch.

When making your next crossed stitch, make sure you skip a stitch. It can look like the first stitch you used to start the cross is the one you need to skip, but it's not.

This shows the skipped stitch (silver needle) and next stitch to work into (red needle).

❋ *Nimue's Counsel*

> **To make sure you're in the right spot as you go, the corner stitches are always worked into 2 stitches that were made in a cluster stitch.**

Round 4

Nothing too hard about this round. All you need to keep an eye on is the chain spaces. Make sure they are only either side of the stitches worked into the 4 crosses along the sides.

When working between the crossed stitches, go between the posts. You're not working into a stitch as you normally would.

Work your between-the-stitches stitch where the red needle is, not where the silver needle is.

Round 5

This one is easy. A stitch in every stitch and chain space with the corners being a stitch, chain 2 and another stitch worked into the 2-chain corner spaces.

 Nimue's Counsel

Remember to pop a stitch marker in the first stitch as you make it so you can easily identify it when you need to join the end of the round.

 Nimue's Counsel

Pop a scrap of yarn in the corner gap before you join it. This will help with the next round.

Round 6

All of the stitches in this round are a not so common stitch, but it's easy once you know how. All you do is yarn over twice, insert your hook in the stitch or space, pull a loop through to the front, yarn over, pull through 2 loops on the hook then yarn over and pull through all 3 loops on the hook. Job done.

If you put a scrap of yarn in the gap of Round 5, it shows you where to work the last stitch of this round.

 *Nimue's Counsel*

If you are working false stitches instead of starting chains, work the false stitch by pulling up a slightly longer loop at the beginning.

Round 7

You don't need my help for this round, but I do have a trick for you at the end of each square.

As you need to make 2 strips of 5 squares and 2 strips of 7 squares, you can join them into strips as you go. When you are up to joining the last round of your second square, chain 1, and join with a double crochet/single crochet (UK/US). Don't cut the yarn. Hold your first square on top – right sides together – and join over the joining stitch and into the 2-chain corner space of the finished square then join as usual. Block your strips before joining them to the centre piece.

Nimue
Round by Round Help

Round 50

Now we've made it through the barrier between Avalon and the real world, it's time to finish our quest for Nimue.

The first round is a simple one, where we work a stitch into every stitch, chain space and join of the Caltha squares.

This photo shows where to poke your hook to work a stitch into the join.

This photo shows the stitches in the 2-chain spaces and join as well as the stitches.

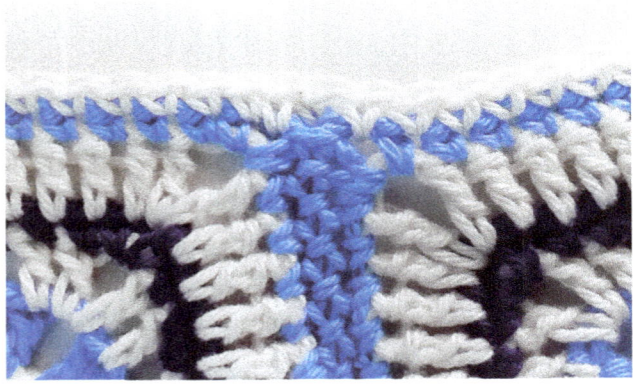

Round 51

Another couple of easy rounds – just a stitch in every stitch and corners are one stitch, chain 2 and one stitch.

Round 52

Round 53

Now it's time to start another fun bit. It's easy.

The corners are simply one stitch in the 2-chain spaces. At the start and the end of the sides, you will skip 3 stitches. Along the edges, you will work 7 stitches in one stitch, skip 2, then a small stitch in the next stitch. Skip 2, work 7 stitches in the next stitch and repeat along the side.

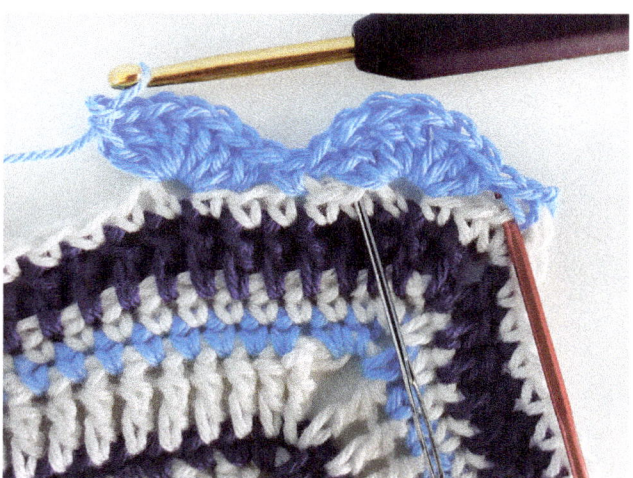

The red needle is in the first of the 3 stitches skipped at the start of the side, and the silver is in the first of the 2 skipped once you start the side.

Round 54

This round will feel familiar as we have done this stitch combination before. Last time it was just at the start and end of the sides of Round 41. This time we work the repeat all the way along the sides, while the corners are again one stitch.

Work a front post stitch around every stitch along the side, with the ones in the dips between the shells as small front post stitches.

Round 55

Here's where we deviate from the stitch pattern we have done before. In this round, all stitches along the sides are worked into the Round 53 stitches, behind the front post stitches of Round 54. The corners, however, are worked into the corner stitches of Round 54.

We are going back to straight sides, so there are different stitches worked along the sides. The start and end of the sides are slightly different to between the shells. At the start you will work a single stitch into the first Round 53 stitch behind. Remember the tip to fold the front post stitches towards you to make the Round 53 stitches you need to work into easier to see.

Then you begin the side repeat, working a half stitch into the next stitch, a small stitch into the next 3 stitches and another half stitch before working the next 3 stitches together.

The needles show the first and last stitches to be worked together.

Round 56

This round attaches the tops of the shells of Round 54 to the background and makes them a little pointy.

The corners and either side of them are easy. When you get to the first shell of Round 54, you will be poking your hook into the "lbv" – loops behind v – and then in the Round 55 stitch behind it at the same time to make one stitch.

The stitch you need to poke into the lbv of is the middle one of the 7-stitch shell, the 4th one.

After that, you work a stitch in the next 2 stitches, then work a front post stitch around the next one, which will be the 3-together stitch.

Then you work a stitch in the next 2 stitches before you're back to the lbv and next stitch at the same time.

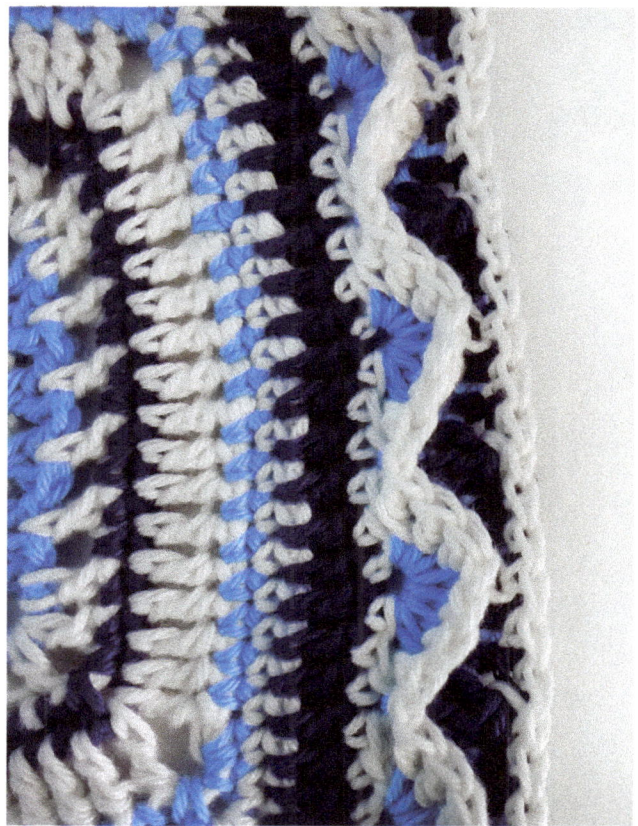

Round 57

Remember way back in Round 29 where we made crossed stitches? Well, in this round we'll also be making cross stitches but this time, there will be 3 stitches in each cross.

Before you begin your first cross, you need to skip 3 stitches. I have broken up the skip instruction though, as you need to skip an extra one at the start of the side.

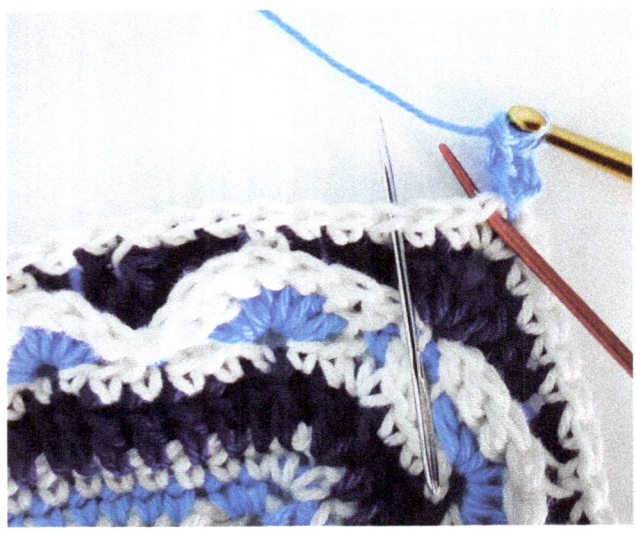

The red needle is the in the first stitch of the side that you need to skip before you start the repeats of crosses. The silver needle is in the first stitch you need to work a stitch into.

The red needle is still in the first stitch of the side, the silver needle is where you work the second stitch of the first cross.

The red needle is still in the first stitch of the side, the silver is in the stitch where you work the 3rd stitch of the first cross.

Then, you're off, skipping 2 stitches before starting your next cross.

✳ *Nimue's Counsel*

Make sure you are skipping 2 unused stitches! It can look like the stitch you used for the first stitch of your cross has not been worked.

The first stitches of the crosses should always be in the front posts and stitches in the lbv.

The last cross begins in the last stitch of the side.

Round 58

An easy enough round to do! This time, when you work stitches between stitches, it's not in the middle of crossed stitches, but between the crosses. Easy!

The red needle shows where to work the first between stitches stitch and the silver the first of the 3 stitches to have one stitch in each.

✳ *Nimue's Counsel*

The first stitch of the 3 to be worked into can be hidden a bit by the stitch between stitches, so pull it to the side if the first stitch is obscured.

Round 59

More fun times of working in other rounds. The first and last stitches of the sides are front post stitches worked around the Round 57 corner stitches.

Then you start the side repeat by doing a half stitch in the stitch that was worked between stitches, so you skip the 2 stitches behind the front post stitches you just worked.

Now it's time to work 3 stitches together, but they are worked as front posts around the Round 57 cross stitches.

Yes, the middle one will be a bit fiddly to work around, but you can do it.

Then, you work a half stitch in the stitch that was worked between crosses before your next front post 3-together stitch.

Round 60

Nothing too hard about this round. The only thing that's a little different is when you get to your front post 3-together stitches. This is where you use the same stitch twice. You work a stitch in it and then around the same stitch as a front post. The red needle shows where to work in and the silver needle where to work the front post.

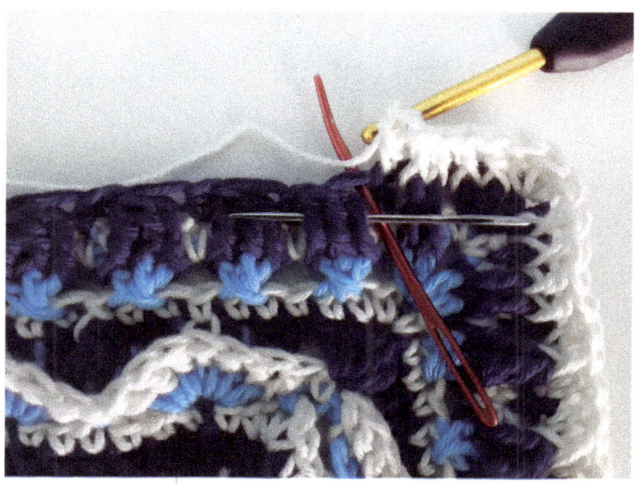

Round 61

We're in familiar territory again with this round, creating shells of 7 stitches along the side. The corners and stitches on either side are easy.

The only thing to note is that there is only one stitch skipped at the start and end of the sides and 2 stitches skipped otherwise. We also begin and end with the small stitch rather than the sets of 7 stitches.

The needle shows where to work your first set of 7 stitches after skipping 2 stitches.

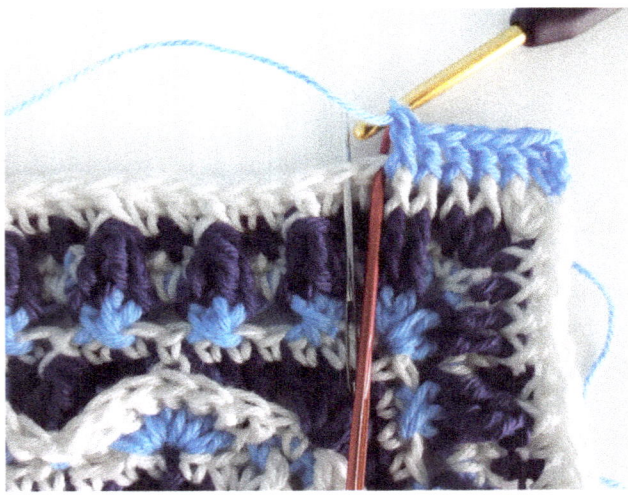

The red needle shows where to work the last small stitch of the side after skipping one stitch.

The red needle shows the single stitch to skip before you work a small stitch where the silver needle is.

Round 62

This round is just like Round 54 along the sides while we continue the front post stitches either side of the corners. So all front post stitches except for the corner ones.

The first and last stitches along the sides after and before the corner front posts is a small front post stitch around the small stitches of Round 61.

Round 63

Again, this round is the same as you've done before, after the front post corner stitches are done. You're working behind Round 62 into the Round 61 stitches. The difference is only at the start and end of the side, where you crochet 2 stitches together.

The needles are in the 2 stitches to work together.

After that, it's all the same as Round 55 with crocheting 3 stitches together in the dips between the shells.

At the end of the shells section, you again crochet 2 together, rather than 3.

The last leg of the 2-together stitch should be in the stitch behind your last small front post stitch.

Round 64

Now we deviate slightly from the path we went down in Round 56. Yes, you are still attaching the shells to the back by using the lbv and next stitch at the same time, but the stitches between those are a little different.

Instead of working a front post stitch around the 3-together stitch, you work 2 stitches into it. All other stitches have just one worked in them.

The red needle shows the stitch to work 2 stitches into.

Round 65

Well done! Time to take a breather with the next 3 rounds. You've done it all before. Stitch in every stitch with one stitch, chain 2, one stitch corners.

Round 66

Small stitches this time.

Round 67

And back to regular stitches...

Round 68

Now we begin the last interesting section before the border!

Nothing hard, just alternating between front post stitches and half stitches along the side, starting and ending with front post stitches.

The red needle shows where to work the first front post stitch and the silver, where to work the first half stitch.

Round 69

Now for a fun one! You'll be fine with the corners, as you've done the same before.

Once you start the side, there is a really long instruction, but it's not hard to do. You will be using the same stitch twice a couple of times in each small repeat.

After you've done your corner and skipped one stitch, it's time to start the side repeat. The first thing you do is work a stitch in the next 2 stitches. Then, you will be using the same stitch you worked the last stitch into as the first of 5 stitches for the next part.

These 5 stitches – front post, half stitch, front post, half stitch, front post are used and skipped to create one stitch.

Once you have worked your front post 3-together stitches, you need to work a stitch in the same stitch that the last leg the together stitch was worked around - where the silver needle is pointing in the photo.

At the end of the side, there is one stitch worked in a stitch followed by a front post stitch before you skip 1 stitch and work the corner.

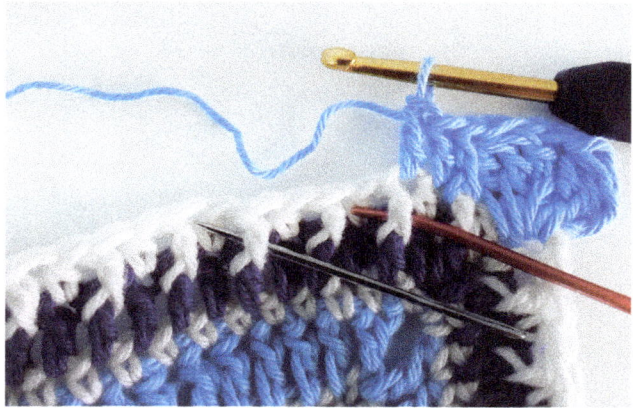

The red needle is under the first of the 5 stitches and the silver is under the last stitch of the 5. You will be using the 3 front post stitches to crochet a 3-together stitch. Those 3 stitches that make up the together stitch are also worked as front post stitches. You won't be using the 2 half stitches between the front posts.

Round 70

And now for an easier round! Along the sides after your front post stitch there is a stitch worked in the next 2 stitches before you begin the side repeat. You will be skipping the front post 3-together stitches and working a stitch in the 3 stitches between them and chaining 2.

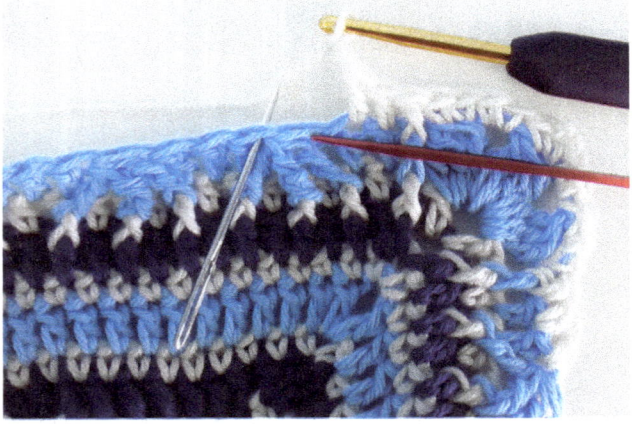

The red needle is in the stitch to be skipped and the silver in the first of the 3 stitches to be worked into.

At the end of the side repeat, there are 2 stitches worked instead of 3, then a front post stitch before you work to the corner.

Round 71

More fun times in this round! It's easy up to the start of the side repeat.

After your front post stitch and a stitch in the next stitch, you will be working 2 large stitches with chain 2 between them into the front post 3-together stitch from Round 70, in front of the 2-chain space of Round 71. Then you need to chain 2 again and this time work a front post large stitch around the same front post 3-together stitch.

The red needle shows where to work the 2 large stitches separated by a 2-chain space. The silver needle above and the red needle in the next photo shows where to work the front post stitch after your chain 2.

 *Nimue's Counsel:*

Make sure you work in front of the 2-chain space as we use it in the next round.

This is where to work the front post stitch.

Then you need to skip 1 stitch, the 2-chain space and another stitch. Those are the Round 70 stitches behind the 3 you just made, so the next stitch is worked into the middle of the set of 3 Round 70 stitches.

The needles show where the next 3 stitches in/around are worked after the stitch in the middle of the set of 3 stitches.

Round 72

The corners, start and end of rounds are easy. Along the sides, you will be working behind the stitches of the last round into the stitches and chain spaces of Round 70 as well as into the small stitches between your 3-stitch fan shapes.

The needles are in the 2 stitches of Round 70 with the 2-chain space you need between them. I have folded the fan shape to the front to expose them.

The needle here is showing where to work into the stitch of Round 71.

Round 73

I promise you, this is the last fiddly round. From here on in, it's plain sailing.

After your corner, the stitches before the side repeat are easy. Now, we will be using the "lbv" – loop behind v – of the middle large stitch of the 3-stitch fan shapes of Round 71 on its own. Last time we used a similar stitch, we also used the next stitch of the previous round. Not this time.

Here is where you work a stitch into the lbv of that middle fan stitch.

✳ *Nimue's Counsel*

> **You will know you are keeping on track if your stitch into the lbv is worked after you have done a stitch in the first 2 of the 4 worked behind Round 71 in the last round. The middle stitch of the 5 worked in a row should be in the stitch that is between the fans.**

Round 74

An easy enough round. All you need to do is work 2 stitches together at some points along the side. Note that the start and end of the sides are not symmetrical.

At the start of the side, you begin with crocheting 2 stitches together, then work a stitch in the next 10 stitches.

The first stitch of the 2 you will be crocheting together will always be the one worked into the lbv of the fan stitch as shown by the red needle.

The last crochet 2-together begins in the last stitch in the fan. After that, you simply work a stitch in the 11 remaining side stitches before working your corner.

Round 75

Time to take a breather with a simple stitch in every stitch round. You know the drill by now.

Round 76

And once more, with small stitches this time.

Round 77

Now it's time to start the border. Almost there.

The only thing to note here is that the corners are 2 stitches, chain 2 and then 2 more stitches.

Along the sides, you are chaining 1, skipping 1 stitch, then working a stitch in the next 2 stitches. You should finish the side by chaining and skipping 1 stitch.

 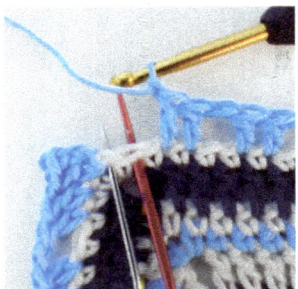

Round 78

Another easy one with just front post stitches worked along the sides around every stitch with a chain between them. You skip the 1-chain spaces. We are back to 1 stitch, chain 2 and 1 stitch corners again.

Round 79

This round is the same as the last round, except there are 3 front post stiches at the start and the end of the sides.

Round 80

And the same again, but with 4 front post stitches at the start and end of the sides.

Round 81

Here's where we make the pointy bits at the top of the fence posts. The start and end of the sides are slightly different to the middle of the sides.

At the start and end of the sides, you chain 1 and crochet 2 stitches together twice over the 4 front post stitches.

After you have skipped the first 1-chain space, you will work a 3-together stitch over the next 2 stitches and 1-chain space. Here's where to work the first and third leg of the 3-together stitch. Make sure you chain 2 between all of your 3-together stitches.

At the end of the side, you will finish your last 3-together in the last 1-chain space of the side, before you chain 2 and work your two 2-together stitches and chain 1 over the last 4 front post stitches.

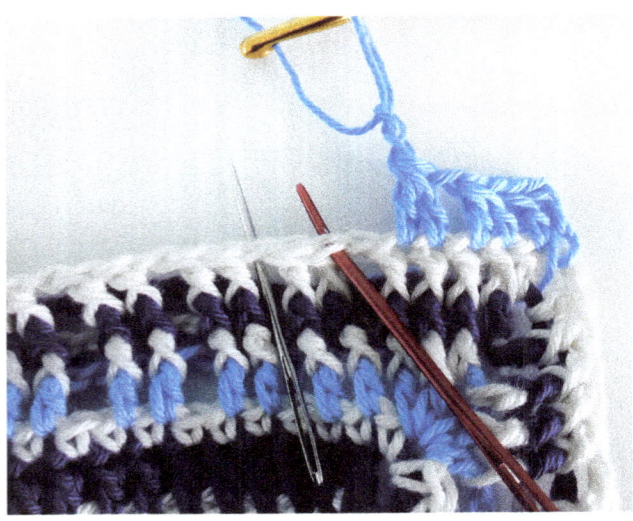

Round 82

And here we are at the very last round!

This one is super easy. A stitch in every stitch and 1-chain space and 2 stitches in every 2-chain space.

✱ *Nimue's Counsel*

If you find your blanket is curling up, try working 3 stitches in the 2-chain spaces. It was flat for me, but if you chain tightly, you may need the extra stitches to make it sit flat.

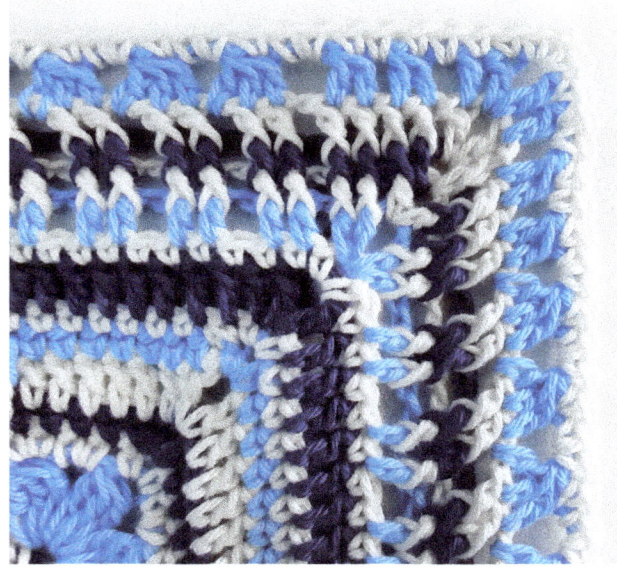

It's time to rest your mounts, unpack your saddle bags and relax.

CONGRATULATIONS!
Your quest for Nimue is complete.

NIMUE'S TIDINGS

Here you will find the miscellany you may need as you negotiate your quest.

Here be the glossary of all stitches and techniques used, the rounds to change colours for Kim's Nimue, the left-handed charts and instructions how to access the help page with video links, among other things.

GLOSSARY

Abbreviations

cnr/s	corner/s	
R	round	
rep	repeat	
sp/s	space/s	
st/s	stitch/es	
stch	starting chain	Used in place of the first st in a round. Is included in st count.
stdg	standing	Attach yarn to your hook with a slip knot then work the st indicated as normal.
yo	yarn over	Wrap yarn over hook from back to front.

Stitches UK/US

·	ss	slip stitch	Insert hook into st or sp indicated, yo and pull through st or sp and loop on hook.
o	ch	chain	yo, pull through loop on hook.
+	dc / sc	double crochet / single crochet	Insert hook into st or sp indicated, yo, pull loop to front, yo, pull through both loops on hook.
T	htr / hdc	half treble crochet / half double crochet	Wrap yarn around hook, insert hook into st or sp indicated, yo, pull loop to front (3 loops on hook), yo, pull through all 3 loops on hook.
T	tr / dc	treble crochet / double crochet	Wrap yarn around hook, insert hook into st or sp indicated, yo, pull loop to front (3 loops on hook), 2x [yo, pull through 2 loops on hook].
T	hdtr / htr	half double treble crochet / half triple crochet	Wrap yarn around hook twice, insert hook into st or sp indicated, yo, pull loop to front (4 loops on hook), yo, pull through 2 loops (3 loops on hook), yo, pull through all 3 loops on hook.
T	dtr / tr	double treble crochet / triple crochet	Wrap yarn around hook twice, insert hook into st or sp indicated, yo, pull loop to front (4 loops on hook), 3x [yo, pull through 2 loops].

Techniques

Symbol	Abbr	Term	Description
		at the same time	Shows where to place your hook when gathering sts from a previous round into one.
		behind	The bend in the post of the st shows it is worked behind previous round/s.
	bp	back post	Insert hook around the post of the st indicated from the back. Can be applied to any st.
	cl	cluster	Numerous sts worked together as one st in the st or sp indicated. Begin the type of st indicated as many times as instructed. Work each st of the cl up to before the last yo and pull through 2 loops on hook, then yo and pull though all loops on hook. Could be any number of any kind of st. e.g. 4trcl, 5dtrcl, 3htrcl and worked as fp or bp.
	fp	front post	Insert hook around the post of the st indicated from the front. Can be applied to any st.
		in front	The bend in the post of the st shows it is worked in front of previous round/s.
	inv join	invisible join	Cut yarn after completing last st of round. Pull tail up through the last st, thread tail onto needle, insert needle under "v" of first true st of the round and back through the centre of the last st, and through the lbv of the last st. Pull tight enough to form a "v" on top of the stch, weave end away.
	lbv	loop behind v	The third loop or back bump of a st on the back. It's located under the back loop of a st. Any st can be worked into lbv, including cl and tog sts.
	mc	magic circle	Method used to begin a square. Wrap yarn around a few fingers, forming a loop, insert your hook into the centre and pull the working yarn through, ch1 to secure. Work R1 sts into the ring, pull the tail to close the ring once all sts have been made and secure by weaving the end in well.
	tog	together	Numerous sts worked together as one st over a number of sts or sps as indicated. Work the specified number of sts up to before the last yo and pull through 2 loops on hook, then yo and pull though all loops on hook. "tog" will be followed by "over next # sts". It can be done with different numbers and types of sts. e.g. tr5tog over next 5 sts, dc2tog over next 2 sts. Can be worked as fp or bp.

Avalon
Left-handed Charts

See page 36 for right-hand versions of the charts.

Avalon Rounds 1 - 22

Avalon Rounds 22 - 33

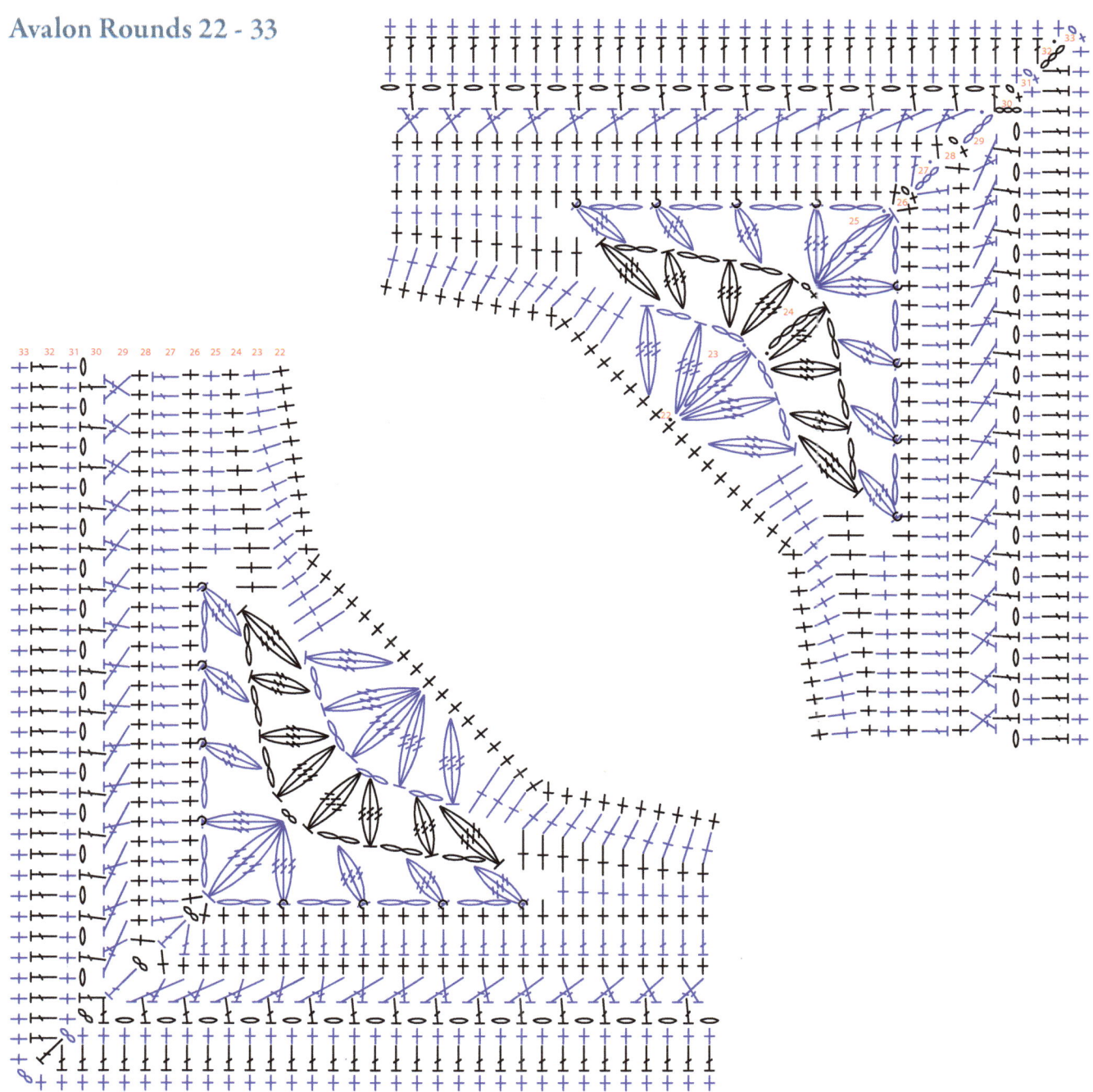

Avalon Rounds 33 - 49

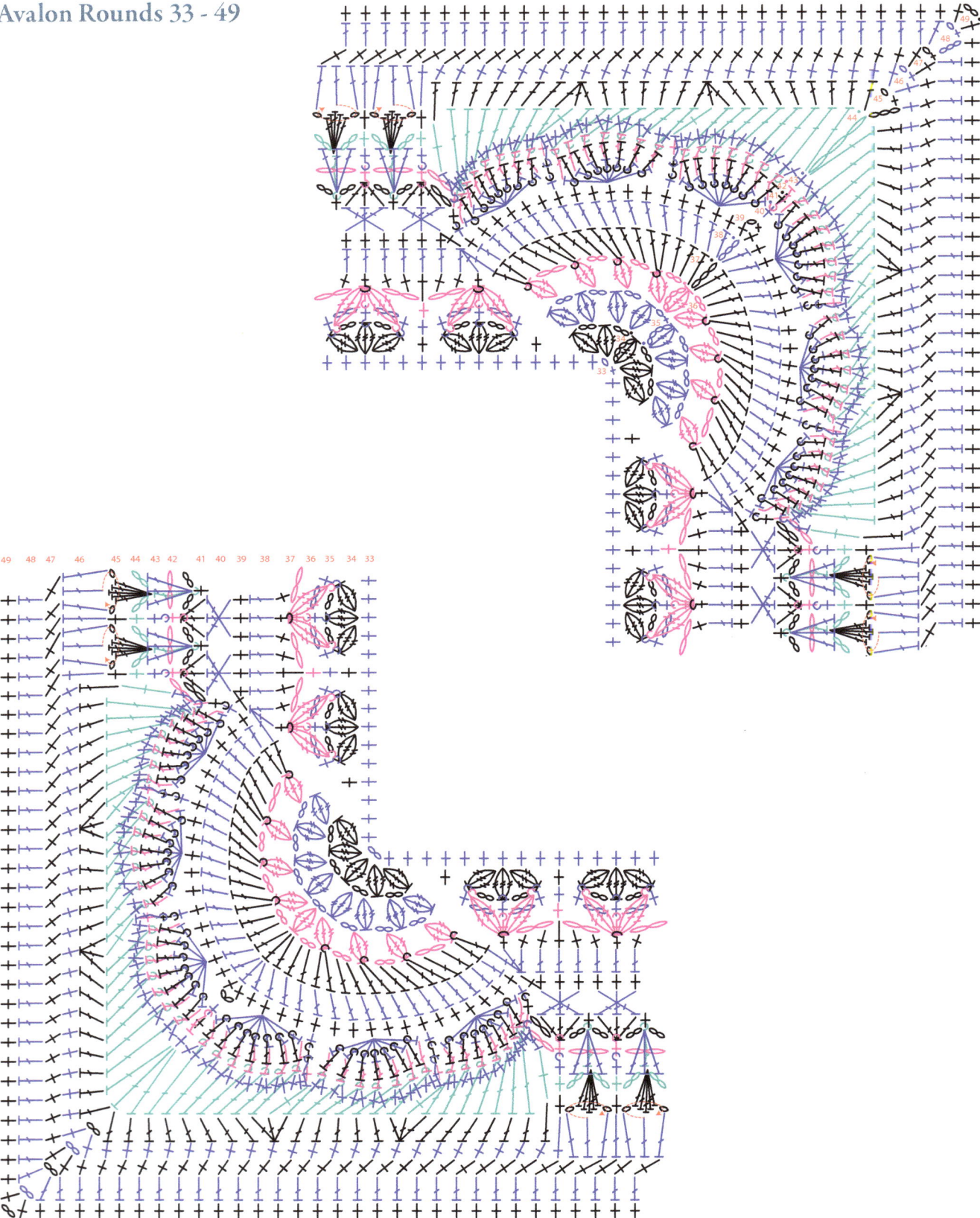

Caltha
Left-handed Chart

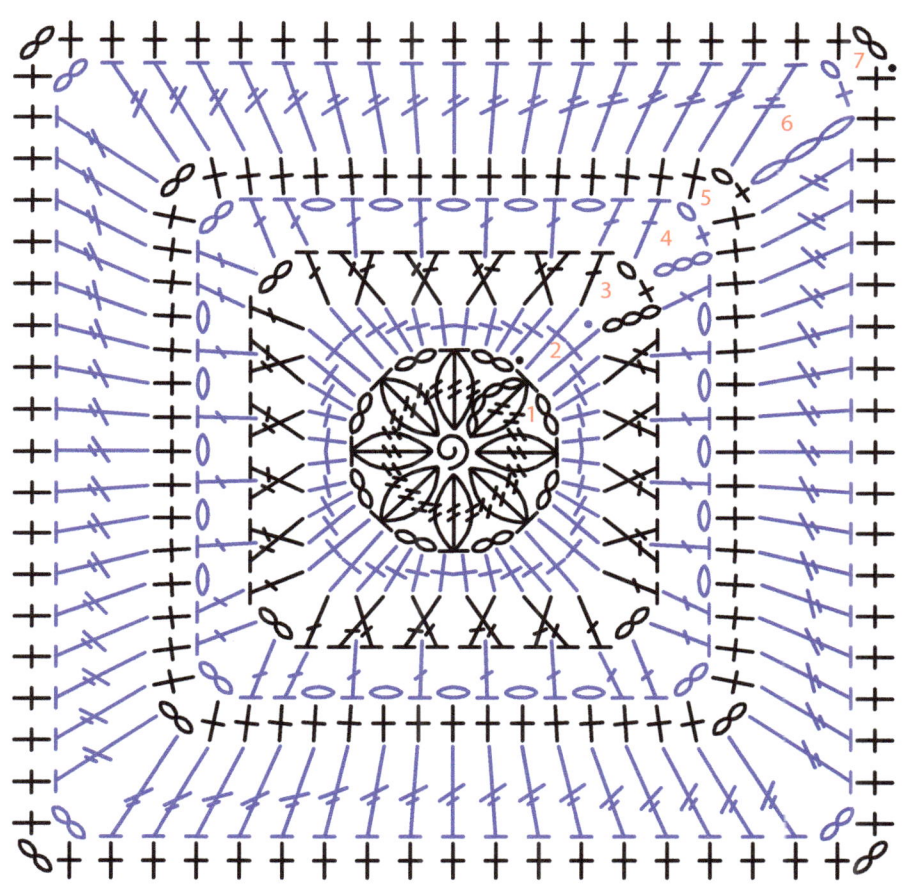

Nimue
Left-handed Charts

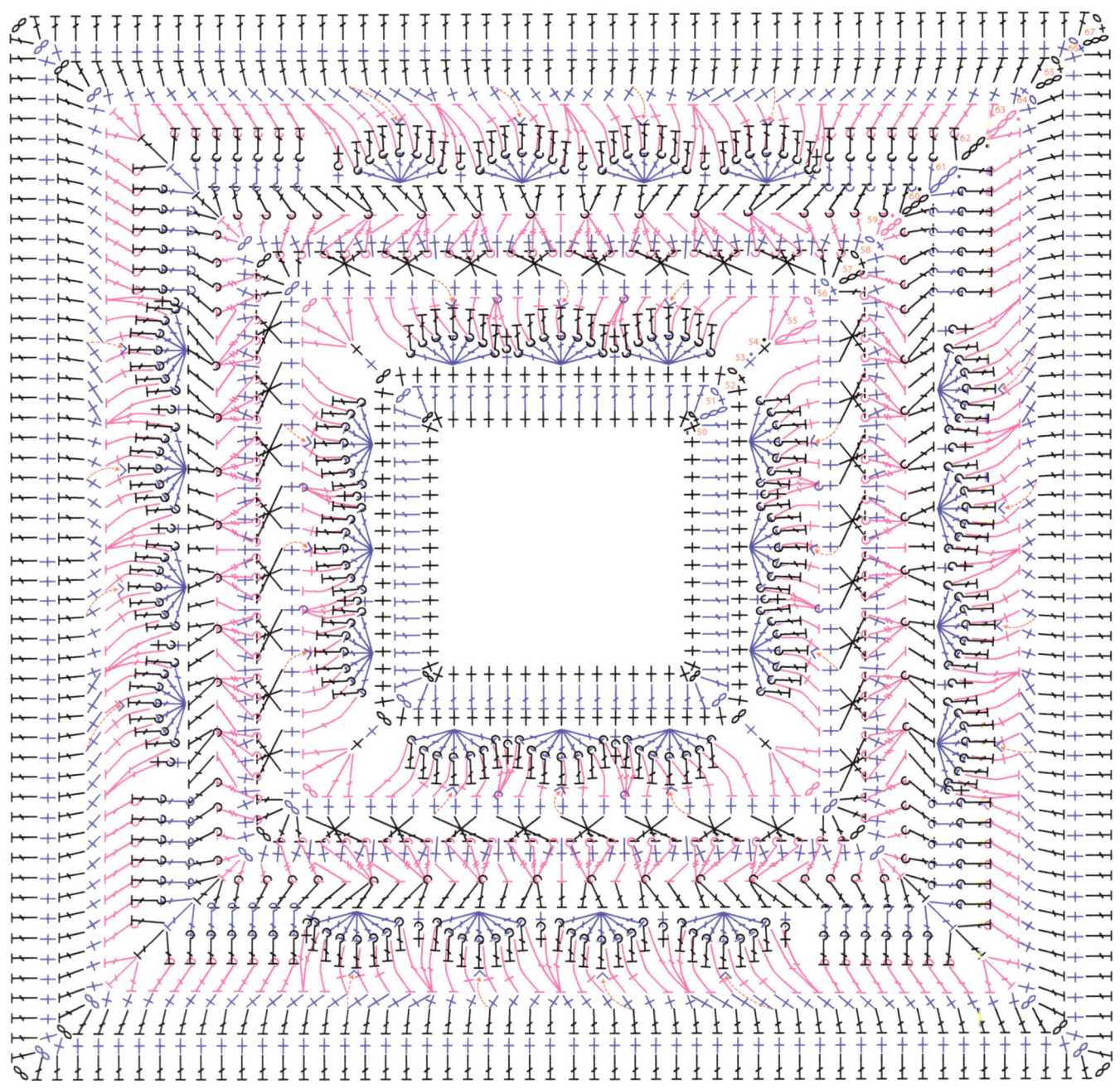

Nimue Rounds 50 - 67

Nimue Rounds 67 - 82

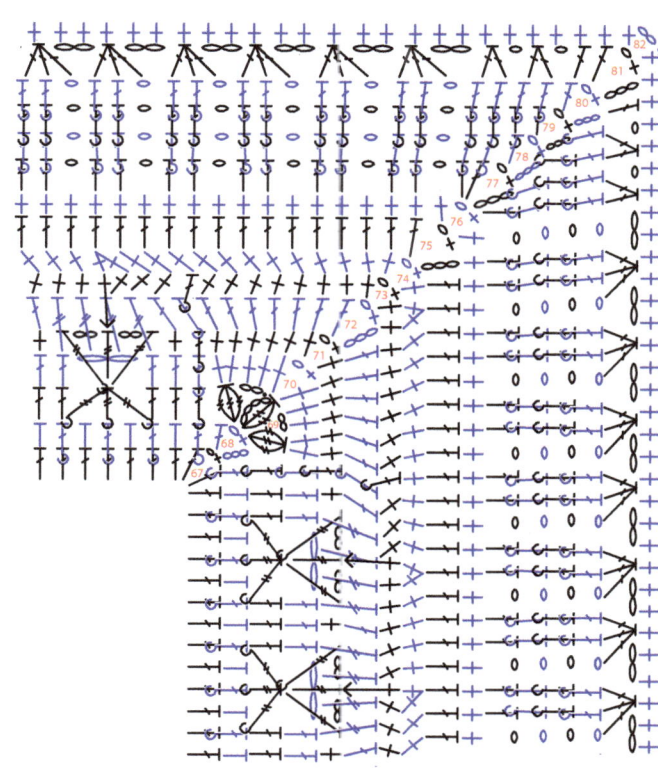

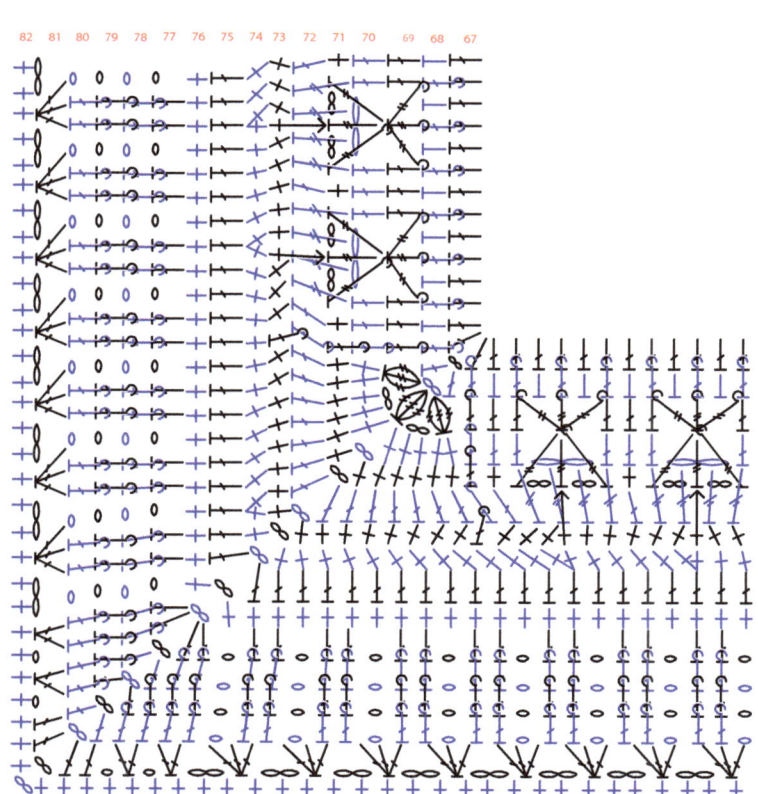

Kim's Nimue Colour Changes

Avalon

Rounds	Colour
1	Peach
2-3	Hot Pink
4-5	Parchment
6-7	Pink Rose
8	Hot Pink
9	Daffodil
10-12	Parchment
13-14	Pink Rose
15	Hot Pink
16-17	Parchment
18	Pink Rose
19	Hot Pink
20-28	Parchment
29	Peach
30	Pink Rose
31-33	Parchment
34	Hot Pink
35	Pink Rose
36	Daffodil
37-39	Parchment
40-42	Pink Rose
43	Peach
44-45	Daffodil
46-49	Parchment

Caltha V1 – make 12

Rounds	Colour
1	Peach
2	Hot Pink
3	Pink Rose
4-7	Parchment

Caltha V2 – make 12

Rounds	Colour
1	Hot Pink
2	Peach
3	Pink Rose
4-7	Parchment

Nimue

Rounds	Colour
50-52	Parchment
53	Daffodil
54	Pink Rose
55-56	Parchment
57	Peach
58	Parchment
59	Hot Pink
60	Parchment
61	Daffodil
62	Pink Rose
63-67	Parchment
68	Pink Rose
69	Peach
70	Parchment
71	Hot Pink
72	Pink Rose
73-77	Parchment
78	Pink Rose
79	Daffodil
80	Peach
81	Pink Rose
82	Hot Pink

HELPFUL LINKS

I have created a page on my website for you to make accessing the videos and other information easy. Type in this link into your web browser (or click the link in the digital version once you download it) https://shelleyhusbandcrochet.com/nimue-helpful-links/

On that page you'll find:

>> links to the right-handed and mirrored videos,

>> general helpful links,

>> links to short videos showing common stitches and techniques, including joining, magic circle and false stitch, and

>> a link to my Facebook group should you need more help.

If you are still having any trouble, please don't hesitate to reach out. You can email me from my website, shelleyhusbandcrochet.com.

Digital Download

Scan the QR code to download the digital version of this book.

THANK YOU

So many folks helped make Nimue possible. If you have any of my other books, you will recognise many of the names here.

Thanks, Michelle Lorimer, for your graphic design skills once again.
We almost don't have to talk these days to make the ideas come to life.
Love your work.

Thank you, Jo O'Keefe, for the fabulous photography, making the photos look like they were taken in a cool misty forest instead of the middle of an Aussie summer.

Thank you, SiewBee Pond, for yet again lending your eyes and brain to work your technical editing and proofreading skills.

Thanks to Amy Gunderson, for always being willing to take on a big charting challenge.

New to the team for this pattern, Regine Oswald checked all the charts for me. Thank you, Regine.

Thank you, Kim Siebenhausen for coming up with the colour scheme and making the pinks sample for me. And Samantha Taylor, for making the luxury sample for me.

My pattern testing team were super keen to take on the huge commitment of testing Nimue. Thank you, Anna Moore, Bonita Dunne, Chris Wilkins, Judy Hartwig, Kathy Mant, Lyn Merton, Marion Van Steveninck, Melissa Russell, Ruth Bracey, Samantha Taylor.

Thank you to Bendigo Woollen Mills for supplying the yarn for three of the samples.

And lastly, thank you for choosing to go on a crochet adventure with my Nimue. I hope you enjoy every moment.

ABOUT THE AUTHOR

Shelley Husband is a prolific crochet pattern designer, publishing 6 books bursting with modern takes on the traditional granny square. Her first book, Granny Square Flair, won the best crochet book of 2019 in the UK.

Shelley has a real passion for designing seamless crochet patterns with the aim of teaching others through encouragingly supported patterns to create timeless, classic crochet heirlooms.

Based on Gunditjmara country also known as Narrawong in South West Victoria, Australia, when not designing and publishing new patterns, Shelley teaches crochet in person around Australia, and throughout the world via her online presence.

You can find Shelley online on her website shelleyhusbandcrochet.com.

MORE BOOKS
by Shelley Husband

Granny Square Academy
Learn all there is to know about making granny squares, including how to read patterns.

Granny Square Academy 2
Expand your granny square knowledge with instructions for more advanced stitches and techniques.

Granny Square Flair
50 written and charted granny square patterns and 11 project ideas to make with them.

Beneath the Surface
A beginner friendly pattern, with lots of extra support including video links.

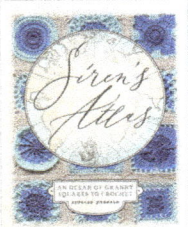
Siren's Atlas
64 written and charted granny square patterns for adventurous crocheters.

Granny Square Patchwork
40 written and charted granny squares patterns of 6 sizes and 12 projects to make with them.

Dotty Spotty
Classic circle-to-square granny square fun.

The Cove
A pick your path pattern inspired by coastal adventures.

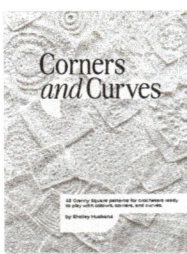
Corners and Curves
45 Granny Square patterns for crocheters ready to play with colours, corners and curves.

Buy my books direct from me in my shop or online at most online book retailers around the world. Visit my pattern shop for digital patterns galore.

shop.shelleyhusbandcrochet.com

www.ingramcontent.com/pod-product-compliance
Lightning Source LLC
Chambersburg PA
CBHW061807290426
44109CB00031B/2958